Building the GOVERNANCE PARTNERSHIP

The Chief Executive's Guide to Getting the Best from the Board

SECOND EDITION

Sherill K. Williams *and*
Kathleen A. McGinnis

BOARDSOURCE®
Building Effective Nonprofit Boards

Library of Congress Cataloging-in-Publication Data

Williams, Sherill K.

Building the governance partnership : the chief executive's guide to getting the best from the board / by Sherill K. Williams and Kathleen A. McGinnis.

    p. cm. -- (The governance series)

Prev. ed. published under title: Getting the best from your board.

Includes bibliographical references.

ISBN 1-58686-124-7

1. Nonprofit organizations--Management. 2. Boards of directors. 3. Chief executive officers. I. McGinnis, Kathleen A. II. Williams, Sherill K. Getting the best from your board. III. BoardSource (Organization) IV. Title.

HD62.6.W56 2011

658.4'22--dc22   2011007614

Published by BoardSource
750 9th Street, NW, Suite 650
Washington, DC 20001

BOARDSOURCE®
Building Effective Nonprofit Boards

BoardSource is dedicated to advancing the public good by building exceptional nonprofit boards and inspiring board service.

BoardSource was established in 1988 by the Association of Governing Boards of Universities and Colleges (AGB) and Independent Sector (IS). Prior to this, in the early 1980s, the two organizations had conducted a survey and found that although 30 percent of respondents believed they were doing a good job of board education and training, the rest of the respondents reported little, if any, activity in strengthening governance. As a result, AGB and IS proposed the creation of a new organization whose mission would be to increase the effectiveness of nonprofit boards.

With a lead grant from the Kellogg Foundation and funding from five other donors, BoardSource opened its doors in 1988 as the National Center for Nonprofit Boards with a staff of three and an operating budget of $385,000. On January 1, 2002, BoardSource took on its new name and identity. These changes were the culmination of an extensive process of understanding how we were perceived, what our audiences wanted, and how we could best meet the needs of nonprofit organizations.

Today, BoardSource is the premier voice of nonprofit governance. Its highly acclaimed products, programs, and services mobilize boards so that organizations fulfill their missions, achieve their goals, increase their impact, and extend their influence. BoardSource is a 501(c)(3) organization.

BoardSource provides

- resources to nonprofit leaders through workshops, training, and an extensive Web site (www.boardsource.org)

- governance consultants who work directly with nonprofit leaders to design specialized solutions to meet an organization's needs

- the world's largest, most comprehensive selection of material on nonprofit governance, including a large selection of books and CD-ROMs

- an annual conference that brings together approximately 900 governance experts, board members, and chief executives and senior staff from around the world

For more information, please visit our Web site at www.boardsource.org, e-mail us at mail@boardsource.org, or call us at 800-883-6262.

Have You Used These BoardSource Resources?

THE GOVERNANCE SERIES

1. *Ten Basic Responsibilities of Nonprofit Boards, Second Edition*
2. *Legal Responsibilities of Nonprofit Boards, Second Edition*
3. *Financial Responsibilities of Nonprofit Boards, Second Edition*
4. *Fundraising Responsibilities of Nonprofit Boards, Second Edition*
5. *The Nonprofit Board's Role in Mission, Planning, and Evaluation, Second Edition*
6. *Structures and Practices of Nonprofit Boards, Second Edition*

OTHER BOOKS

Govern More, Manage Less: Harnessing the Power of Your Nonprofit Board, Second Edition

The Nonprofit Chief Executive's Ten Basic Responsibilities

The Board Chair Handbook, Second Edition

Chief Executive Succession Planning: Essential Guidance for Boards and CEOs, Second Edition

Chief Executive Transitions: How to Hire and Support a Nonprofit CEO

Nonprofit Executive Compensation: Planning, Performance, and Pay, Second Edition

Taming the Troublesome Board Member

Trouble at the Top: The Nonprofit Board's Guide to Managing an Imperfect Chief Executive

Meeting, and Exceeding Expectations: A Guide to Successful Nonprofit Board Meetings, Second Edition

Driving Strategic Planning: A Nonprofit Executive's Guide, Second Edition

Culture of Inquiry: Healthy Debate in the Boardroom

Governance as Leadership: Reframing the Work of Nonprofit Boards

The Nonprofit Board Answer Book: A Practical Guide for Board Members and Chief Executives, Second Edition

The Handbook of Nonprofit Governance

Who's Minding the Money? An Investment Guide for Nonprofit Board Members, Secoond Edition

The Board Building Cycle: Nine Steps to Finding, Recruiting, and Engaging Nonprofit Board Members, Second Edition

The Source: Twelve Principles of Governance That Power Exceptional Boards

Fearless Fundraising for Nonprofit Boards, Second Edition

Navigating the Organizational Lifecycle: A Capacity-Building Guide for Nonprofit Leaders

Understanding Nonprofit Financial Statements, Third Edition

The Nonprofit Dashboard: A Tool for Tracking Progress

Better Bylaws; Creating Effective Rules for Your Nonprofit Board, Second Edition

Managing Conflicts of Interest: A Primer for Nonprofit Boards, Second Edition

The Nonprofit Policy Sampler, Second Edition

DVDs

Meeting the Challenge: An Orientation to Nonprofit Board Service

Speaking of Money: A Guide to Fundraising for Nonprofit Board Members

ONLINE ASSESSMENTS

Board Self-Assessment

Assessment of the Chief Executive

Executive Search — Needs Assessment

For an up-to-date list of publications and information about current prices, membership, and other services, please call BoardSource at 800-883-6262 or visit our Web site at www.boardsource.org. For consulting services, please e-mail us at consulting@boardsource.org or call 877-892-6293.

CONTENTS

ACKNOWLEDGMENTS

The authors wish to thank Richard Moyers, Vice President for Programs and Communications at the Eugene and Agnes E. Meyer Foundation in Washington, D.C., for editorial guidance and creative ideas on the first edition of this book.

Additionally, many thanks to Ellen Hirzy for her time, thought, and care in editing the first edition.

INTRODUCTION

Much that has been written about chief executives and boards repeats a familiar refrain: When it is successful, the relationship is a balancing act — carefully choreographed, but at the same time prepared to shift, respond, and change when the balance seems off-kilter. A nonprofit chief executive manages the staff but is an employee of the board. In a constructive partnership with the board, he or she also provides essential leadership that engages and involves the board in governance. An effective chief executive is the spark that ignites the partnership and helps board performance move from ordinary to extraordinary.

According to BoardSource's *Nonprofit Governance Index 2010,* board work — in and between meetings — consumes a considerable amount of time from paid and volunteer leaders. Chief executives spend an average of 22 hours per month on board and committee work. The larger the board, the more time they spend (21 hours for small boards compared to 27 hours for large boards). Board chairs spend 19 hours and other board members spend 10 hours.

This book offers practical tips and perspectives to help chief executives as they guide this considerable investment of human resources. The qualities of a true partnership with the board — support, trust, honesty, forthrightness, respect, and understanding — must belong to both the chief executive and the board. Just like building any relationship, the process calls for hard work by both parties. But the rewards, including success for the organization and the chief executive, are worth the effort.

For the chief executive, the partnership involves working for, working with, and working the board. Working for the board, the chief executive has specific expectations around vision and accountability to live up to as he or she translates the board's collective thinking into practices and programs that fulfill the organization's mission. Working with the board, the chief executive shares knowledge and information to engage board members in asking the critical strategic questions that contribute to organizational effectiveness. Working the board, he or she primes board members to open doors to resources and relationships that make the organization the best it can be. The partnership between the chief executive and the board focuses on the organization's mission, with both parties bringing their appropriate skills and expertise to bear on the desired results.

This book offers seven rules for the chief executive to lead by, and to follow:

1. Make mission matter. Cultivate the board's passion for the mission; board members will be excited about the organization's work and dedicated to the cause.

2. Know the organization. Inspire the board's confidence by understanding the organization from the inside out — history, organizational culture, public perceptions, and community context.

3. Cultivate relationships. It's up to the chief executive to build habits and interactions that engage and involve the board in a constructive partnership.

4. Inform and communicate. Prepare board members for success by absorbing information, sharing it, and understanding the magic of real communication.

5. Facilitate a balance in roles and responsibilities. Clearly articulated expectations and constructive feedback help both board members and the chief executive hold up their ends of the partnership.

6. Structure the board's work. When the chief executive provides board members with an understanding of the organization and a process for the board's activities, it is easier for board members to be fully involved.

7. Plan for transitions. Have a plan in place and resources to turn to when either the board chair or chief executive position vacates. This allows the organization to keep the focus on the mission versus the crisis of leadership.

The board chair plays a critical role in developing a successful partnership between the executive and the board. Because open communication between the board chair and the chief executive is essential, each chapter of this book includes two first-person essays related to aspects of the chapter's theme: one from a board chair's perspective and one from a chief executive's. The chair's perspectives provide the board angle regarding specific topics, so that chief executives might take away a lesson or tip for the future in understanding why the board thinks or acts in a certain way. The chief executive's stories offer personal experiences from the field to bring the issues in each chapter to life.

CHAPTER 1
MAKE MISSION MATTER

Cultivate the board's passion for the mission.

Effective chief executives want to make a difference. They enjoy working to help others and to build community partnerships. They are willing to take initiative and even some risk for a cause they believe is important. Through their passion and commitment, they inspire others to give and to follow. They may have been born with these values and qualities, influenced by family or faith, or inspired by mentors. Or they may have experienced a life change that led them into nonprofit work.

Ideally, chief executives come to an organization with a strong personal connection to its cause. But some chief executives may not have that built-in passion when they take on their leadership roles. While many people deliberately choose a nonprofit career because they want rewarding work with a positive impact, some may not have a particular organization or issue in mind. If the chief executive's path to the top job or identification with the cause hasn't generated a deeply felt passion for the mission, he or she must develop it. Such a passion is essential to building shared direction and commitment with the board.

WHY IS PASSION FOR THE MISSION IMPORTANT?

Human beings have an uncanny way of sensing when dedication or passion is missing in their leaders. Passion generates enthusiasm and momentum when pursuing a common goal. Board members who work with a chief executive who shows little excitement about the organization's work are likely to mirror that attitude. Lacking incentive and direction, their work will feel like uninspired drudgery.

When a chief executive accepts a position for financial reasons, to feel important, to appease the board when no other talent is available, or because there were no better job options, his or her motivations eventually become apparent — as obvious as if a bumper sticker were plastered across the executive's forehead, which reads "Marking Time." The chief executive's bumper sticker should say "Save the Whales," "Feed the Children," "Help the Homeless," or "Find the Cure." It must come from the heart and soul, each and every day. If the chief executive's primary personal motivation is anything other than achieving the mission, this conflict of commitment will make it difficult to engage the board and move the organization forward. Because an effective chief executive weighs every action against mission to determine if the resources invested are consistent with the cause, anything less than total focus on mission will also weaken decision making about priorities and programs.

WHERE DOES IT COME FROM?

The chief executive can't expect the board, the staff, or some other source to inspire passion for the mission. Passion is something we generate ourselves and instill in our value system and behaviors.

Start by finding real personal meaning in the mission.

- Go out into the field and meet people who have benefited from the organization's services.

- Befriend a few clients. Touch base regularly. Keep up with what's happening in their lives. Tell their stories and connect their success, at least in part, to the organization.

- Think about close personal parallels when family members or friends have benefited from the work of the organization or a similar one.

- Talk with others on the board and staff who have a personal dedication to the mission. Absorb the impact of their collective experience as a way of building passion for the mission.

Even if you're new to the job and not an expert in the cause, finding a special connection to the mission is key to building the commitment necessary to lead and partner with the board.

KEEPING THE COMMITMENT

Even a seasoned chief executive can lose sight of the mission when the critical tasks of the day — personnel issues, special events, monthly financials, committee meetings, or even broken plumbing — are overwhelming.

Mission can seem incidental when there are so many other plates to spin and challenges to contemplate.

Most chief executives know the feeling of being swallowed up by the minutiae and losing focus on the reason for being. It doesn't lead to the kinds of successes that keep a chief executive going. A perceptive chief executive learns to recognize the signs of a heart aching to find meaning. When you start to lose sight of the mission, an immediate response is called for. Corrective actions might include checking in with one or two client friends or reaching out to board members to talk about big-picture issues. Occasional "mission trips" can help you restore focus on the heart of the organization. Chief executives in need of a trip should dust off their travel guides and try the following ideas:

- Check in with staff and volunteers about recent examples of the organization's impact on people. Remember that stories help give life to statistics and will help folks remember why they are involved with the organization.

- Have conversations with board members about why they feel connected to the mission.

- Participate in some of the organization's services to rejuvenate enthusiasm and stimulate improvement. One organization has set a goal that each board and staff member actively participate in one program activity per year — delivering a health screening, attending a speakers bureau training workshop, taking inventory of client supplies, and making follow-up calls to donors to thank them for their support and ask them what motivates them to support the cause.

- Review the strategic plan. Is it really serving its purpose? Are board members familiar with it, and does the board use the plan in its work? If improvements can be made, working with a small board task force to address the plan's relevance can be a great way to revive passion for the mission in both the chief executive and the board.

CRISIS CAN FAN FLAME OF PASSION

Just as minutiae can pull a chief executive's focus away from what is important, so can challenges that seem overwhelming. The effects of an economic recession often create a spike in need for the organization's services while there is a concurrent downward spike in available resources. In times like this, there are urgent and critical forces that distract the chief executive from her well-laid plans and goals.

In tough times, there is usually a natural tendency to focus on cutting expenses while working to hold on to existing resources. The wise chief executive remembers that expense cuts translate directly into impacts on mission delivery. She understands that this is a good opportunity to work with the board in conducting a program audit that takes into account all the mission-deliverables of the organization and prioritizes them based upon community need, cost-effectiveness in delivery, and other value parameters important to the organization.

The chief executive can prepare the board chair to engage the board in some serious discussions about what programs and services are at the core or heart of the mission — those that literally define the organization — the deal-breakers…and those programs or services that are inefficient or can be put on ice temporarily or permanently without causing long-term damage to the organization or its mission.

One chief executive from a food pantry found that when the economy was down, so were donations. At the same time, needs for the services of the food pantry were on an upward spike due to job layoffs, reductions in salary and loss of benefits among workers in the community. While the mission of the food pantry was to provide nutritional foods to families in need, it had developed several collateral programs along the way including literacy training, nutrition classes, and child day care. Something had to give.

The chief executive prepared a cost-benefit analysis of each of the pantry's services and an environmental scan of other organizations offering similar services. With this mission-related information overlaid with the realities of resource needs, the board decided that it could continue to meet the expanded needs for food if it partnered with other organizations in the community for its literacy and child care programs.

> *While balanced budgets are important, the board can only make the kind of tough fiduciary decisions that it needs to when the information it has at hand is mission-related.*

Another organization was faced with a significant loss of funding due to reprioritizations from a key funder — right as the economic downturn was in full force. The chief executive and the board members all recognized that continuing the existing programs and services in the same manner would just not be possible. But the challenge was how to determine what to cut. To enable logical, educated decisions, the board requested that each program be reviewed formally. The staff leaders prepared summary information including the number of clients served, whether other organizations in the community offered similar services, and the costs associated with the specific offering. By evaluating all programs and services at the same time, it allowed focus on this area and caused the board members to carefully consider if the offering could be done differently. One program was eliminated since there was another entity providing a similar service. One area of service, while not cost-effective, was determined to represent the essence of the organization's mission. The analysis allowed the organization to make the decision to continue in this mission-critical area despite the financial implications, and challenged the development committee of the board to launch a new effort to secure funding for this area of programming.

While balanced budgets are important, the board can only make the kind of tough fiduciary decisions that it needs to when the information it has at hand is mission-related. Tight finances, like very few other situations, gives the chief executive the opportunity to bring focus, understanding, and increased commitment of the board to the organization's mission.

> *Passion for the mission is the beginning of great board involvement, and no influence is as powerful as that of the chief executive.*

SHARING PASSION FOR THE MISSION

The more the chief executive connects with the mission of the organization, the more he or she will tell enthusiastic stories about its positive impact on the community. Passion for the mission makes the executive a valued partner with the board, not just someone who is along for the ride. It shows the executive's human side, so that board members and others will look to him or her for guidance when their family, friends, or colleagues need information or services from the organization.

One must remember that not all board members will be equally as passionate, connected, conversant, or comfortable with the mission. A fervent and engaged chief executive will inspire the same kind of enthusiasm among board members, who will then be more likely to embrace the cause themselves, increasing their commitment, productivity, and effectiveness. To bring passion for the mission into the boardroom, try one or all of the following:

- Share stories with the board about where the organization was in the past and how far it has come. One organization keeps a list of highlights within its history (e.g., date the first Web site was unveiled) and plays a Jeopardy!-style game during board orientation where board members guess the year or decade each highlight took place.

- Research new developments in the field and share them with the board to stimulate discussion about change that the organization may consider.

- Find ways to recognize the work of outstanding volunteers and board members or apply for external awards that honor the organization's accomplishments.

- Use the strategic planning process to reflect on the relevance of the organization's mission. A fresh look at the mission can create increased understanding and commitment of the board to the work of the organization. One organization used humor to set the scene for a fresh look at the mission of the organization by passing out air freshener to each member of their task force and allowing a "puff of fresh air" for each new idea offered in a brainstorming discussion.

> *With increased commitment, productivity, and effectiveness also come solid teamwork and a "we're all in this together" attitude.*

VIEW FROM THE BOARD CHAIR

Passion for the mission is the beginning of great board involvement, and no influence is as powerful as that of the chief executive. We board members, especially in the beginning, take our cues from the culture of the organization and the board. At a first meeting, we pick up on the chief executive's knowledge and enthusiasm. Most board members have busy schedules and many options for board service. If the chief executive comes across as unmotivated, distracted, or lacking in passion for the heart of the organization — its mission — it is difficult for board members to be enthusiastic and it might even call into question the value of our own involvement.

Ideally, board members have a deep passion for the mission when they join the board, but that doesn't always happen. Some join to gain board experience or perhaps to help their careers. Others may be designated representatives from their companies with minimal knowledge of the organization's goals. An effective chief executive recognizes her responsibility to develop board members' emotional commitment, beginning with enticing us to learn about the organization's challenges, objectives, needs, and accomplishments. She needs to tune in to individual motivations so that each board member can see how our unique sets of skills, abilities, and experiences affect the mission.

Astute chief executives keep board members focused on the mission through frequent reminders of accomplishments. Starting or ending meetings with an example of how the organization made a difference can energize people who don't have the opportunity to connect with recipients of the organization's services. Storytelling has tremendous impact and brings facts and figures to life.

One of my favorite experiences that galvanized my passion for one of the organizations I support follows.

At the request of our chief executive, I traveled to Washington, D.C., with a group visiting congressional representatives to advocate for our mission. Our group included some of the organization's clients — including a little boy who had received a vision screening at school and was then referred to an eye care professional. It was discovered that he had a serious condition that jeopardized not only his vision but also his life! While he did lose one eye, he survived and now has resumed the normal activities of many young boys. This little guy's energy and challenge to all of us to "guess which eye is real" had a profound impact on all of us. And I was able to remind one of the representatives that met with us that he voted to establish the funding for the program that discovered the problem — and so he had been part of saving this little boy's life.

Having this experience and sharing the story with others has enabled me to convey my passion for the mission and hopefully inspire others. Our chief executive encourages every board member to participate in these activities so we can each create our own special memory.

In addition to encouraging the board's ability to share the organization's mission, a great chief executive also ensures that board members recognize the value they bring. For maximum engagement, each board member should have a compelling answer for these questions:

- Why me? What can I bring to the organization that will make a real difference?

- Why now? Is the timing right for me to join this board? Can I make the time commitment for the level of participation needed to satisfy both the organization and my own needs?

- Why here? What's special about this organization that will inspire me to contribute?

The answers to these questions are essential in developing passion for the mission. They are so important, in fact, that all chief executives should also be able to answer the questions themselves.

VIEW FROM THE CHIEF EXECUTIVE'S DESK

The patient advocacy trip to Washington, D.C., (see above) came just at the right time. I probably could have passed on having my organization participate. I had a pile of work to do, and I knew how much effort it would take to recruit patients for the three-day trip to lobby for increased research funding for our cause. But I was also feeling that I didn't know what compelled many of our board members to support our organization. I hoped that hearing their personal stories would help me understand their motivation and develop a deeper commitment to our cause.

I started by recruiting the support of our board chair and a staff member who could ask sensitive questions without being threatening. With the board chair's leadership, we invited board members to share their stories. Many initially said that they didn't have one, but in follow-up calls, most realized that our health concern affected co-workers, aging parents, and other family members — and thus affected them, too.

This storytelling project gave us a good opportunity to dig deep into the heart of our mission with our board members. It also gave board members who hadn't yet connected to the mission the impetus to do so. They were eager to sign on to tell their stories on Capitol Hill and help attract more resources to our work. They felt invigorated because they had discovered a new tool to support the organization and bring value to its mission beyond the usual fundraising and meeting attendance responsibilities. They have now developed ongoing relationships with their elected officials by keeping them up to date on our issues and reminding them that our supporters are their constituents.

The sense of excitement was so catching that one board member offered the services of his video company to film the stories so they could be shared at events and board meetings. We now start each meeting with a story from a board member. We also share stories through our fundraising appeals, on our Web site, and in our newsletters.

The storytelling project has expanded to include our donors, many of whom have supported us at modest levels for many years. We discovered that we could tap into their passion for our mission using the opportunity of acknowledging a recent contribution and asking about what compels them to support our organization.

By opening the door to conversation with our donors, we learn about their challenges, their joys, their families, and their careers — past and present. One donor shared that she has supported our mission for 25 years because her favorite aunt was affected by the disease our mission addresses.

Given a common longing for increased connection to the world we live in, a storytelling effort can go a long way toward helping both board members and the community see the organization's mission as a reflection of human experiences, gain comfort in sharing feelings, and develop a culture of understanding built around the mission of the organization.

PARTNERSHIP TIPS TO REMEMBER

- Believe in your organization's mission — your conviction is visible to the board.

- Lead by example — your enthusiasm will be contagious.

- Build and share your passion for the mission by finding and telling your personal stories.

- Challenge board members to find their passion for the organization.

- Don't let mountains or molehills derail your focus from mission-related work.

- Pay attention to signs of mission fatigue and discover avenues to re-energize.

- Build the board's commitment by giving them the scoop on new and emerging trends.

- Keep the strategic plan in mind so mundane issues don't overwhelm or cause the organization to lose focus on what's most important.

- Remember the tremendous impact that storytelling has on bringing facts and figures to life and cementing the commitment of board members who have a personal story to tell. Share stories that deal with the impact on real people.

CHAPTER 2
KNOW THE ORGANIZATION

Inspire confidence by learning and understanding.

Equipped with a passion for the mission, the chief executive must stay ahead of the game. As an important building block in working with the board, he or she needs to know the organization inside and out — past and present, from internal and external perspectives. The chief executive processes every action and every decision through this understanding of what the organization is all about and how it is perceived. This informed approach inspires confidence, engages board members, and supports the board in its own role.

Knowing the organization from the inside means having a good grasp of its history, culture, guiding principles, and values. Knowing it from the outside means being fully aware of external influences, the context for its mission, and public perceptions. In his or her partnership with the board, the chief executive should be the board's link to everyday realities within the organization and among its constituents. For their part, board members support the chief executive by offering access to their community connections and reflections based on their own external perspectives.

The chief executive can learn about the organization's history by visiting long-time board members and former chief executives and staff or by examining annual reports and board minutes.

HONORING THE PAST

Knowing and sharing the history of an organization — its founding story; the mission that people of goodwill joined hands to address; and its major milestones, accomplishments, and challenges — are valuable in connecting the chief executive and board with the past and giving them a sense of how they fit into the future.

The chief executive can learn about the organization's history by visiting long-time board members and former chief executives and staff or by examining annual reports and board minutes. Such actions demonstrate an interest in the people who helped shape the organization, as well as where the organization has been, what it has learned, and how its current strategic direction has developed. Learning the organization's history also shows that the chief executive respects the hard work of his or her predecessors and wants to integrate the contributions of the past into the focus for the future.

Sharing the organization's history can be a routine part of board process and relationships. The chief executive can weave this information into interactions with the board in various ways, including

- focusing on history in board orientation and the board handbook — for example, develop a timeline of the organization's landmark events (such as the launch of its first Web site) from its founding to present time

- asking long-time board members to tell stories about major accomplishments and challenges (It's helpful to hear what has made an impact on them!)

- using stories about organizational history to enrich conversations with donors, prospective supporters, and board members, and to add perspective to formal presentations in the community

- involving past board leaders who are still active supporters and have an eye to the future to join in making board/committee recruitment calls, serve on task forces dealing with special issues, or to speak to the organization's history and journey at the board orientation workshop

Some organizations use the "honorary board member" designation to maintain a link to those whose terms have completed and who have made extraordinary contributions to the cause. This may include keeping the name on the organization's communications materials and inviting them to meetings as nonvoting participants. Additionally they may serve on working committees, task forces, or provide counsel to the chief executive and board chair. These individuals and oftentimes other former board members continue to bring value to the organization in terms of their contacts, their own giving plans, and other links. When individuals have given a significant amount of time to an organization, they generally hope to have been part of a successful entity — and are willing to assist the organization in order to help it remain viable and growing. Think about how to use the talents of these individuals to support future needs.

One organization reached out to its past chief executive and past board chair when it found itself faced with a cash flow crisis and the possibility of a deficit budget. "All hands on deck" were needed and these two leaders helped the new chief executive round up some old friends of the organization and uncover some forgotten treasures — important partnerships, corporate relationships, major donors who had lapsed — just when they were needed the most. Inspired by this success, and the willingness of past leaders to pitch in when the chips were down, the chief executive and board chair formalized an advisory board populated by individuals who had contributed to the organization's success in the past and were willing to continue their support and provide their historical perspective.

UNDERSTANDING ORGANIZATIONAL CULTURE

Every organization has a personality — the shared values and assumptions that are often referred to as organizational culture. Culture is shaped by the organization's history, its view of itself and those it serves, and the people who carry out the work. Every board has its own culture, too — an individual style of operating and decision making that is affected both by tradition and by leadership characteristics.

Culture affects an organization's values, the actions of its leaders, and its approach to mission. For example, a board agenda that is packed with topics with little time for discussion may indicate a culture that values activity over reflection or volume over quality. As another example, consider an organization with a mission to house the homeless. Its culture may reflect the importance of building clients' self-sufficiency through learning and personal achievement in order to end homelessness in the future. Its programs, while fulfilling its basic mission of physically housing those with nowhere else to go, focus on guiding clients toward independence and personal improvement.

> *The chief executive's understanding of organizational culture is important in assessing whether the personality of the organization is well suited to meet current and future needs, and it should be shared with and understood by the board as well.*

The chief executive's understanding of organizational culture is important in assessing whether the personality of the organization is well suited to meet current and future needs, and it should be shared with and understood by the board as well. For a board, organizational culture influences attitudes toward basic responsibilities. Boards that are successful at leading change in an organization have built teamwork, strategic thinking, and informed risk taking into their cultures. The chief executive plays an important role in defining or redefining the culture and values of the organization and helping the board make conscious changes in its culture.

PUTTING CULTURE INTO WORDS

The strategic planning process is a way to understand and/or redefine an organization's culture and values. The first step can be a discovery phase in which the board and key staff determine the principles or values that the organization agrees on, embraces, and uses to guide behavior and actions. Organizational values are a good lens through which to test alternatives for action in everyday behavior or when the organization is facing tough issues.

One organization used the strategic planning process to develop a statement of guiding principles that represent the shared values of board and staff. This statement (on the next page) is included in the volunteer handbook and posted throughout the organization's offices.

CORE VALUES/GUIDING PRINCIPLES

1. Ownership and accountability of the board of directors for the vision of the organization and ownership with volunteer leadership to carry out the steps to reach that vision

2. Teamwork, open communication, trust, and shared understanding among volunteers and staff

3. Maintenance of a solid foundation built on sound business practice and highest ethical and philanthropic standards while operating at peak performance

4. Commitment to and understanding of the mission of the organization and the responsibility it carries in terms of the public's trust

5. Commitment to meaningful involvement and recognition for leadership of all ages and backgrounds who provide philanthropic giving of time, talent, and treasure

6. Continual striving to grow and expand, promoting innovation based on the best data available and maximum outreach to serve populations at highest risk

7. Respect for our community partnerships and action toward collaboration with individuals and organizations that share common goals

8. Excellence in the quality of services and information to internal and external customers

For this organization, when challenging issues arise, one question asked is "does this fit our mission, our vision, and our core values?" An example of how this question impacted the board's actions follows.

An opportunity was presented to the organization that would allow it to take a leadership position on an issue and heighten its image in the community. However, the situation would potentially impact one of its key collaborators and create tension for future endeavors. In considering how to proceed, the organization's value of "respect for community partnerships…" caused it to redirect the opportunity to broaden the involvement of others. While the singular publicity would have been great, the potential long-term negative impact was not worth the risk.

SEARCHING FOR THE RIGHT KIND OF CULTURE

A new chief executive may arrive on the scene to find that all or part of the organizational or board culture is dysfunctional. The organization may have undergone many changes, such as the departure of key staff or dramatic decreases (or increases) in funding. Or weak leadership may have allowed a "free-for-all" or a poorly executed strategic plan. The new chief executive needs to recognize quickly that the pieces are not fitting together in a way that promotes clear direction and maximum harmony. Some signs of dysfunction might be

- staff who do not understand the role of the board or respect its members

- multiple messages from individual messengers about the mission and direction of the organization

- "silo-ed" staff and board work groups that do not communicate or consider the big picture in pursuit of their goals

- a strong need to identify "enemies" inside and outside the organization instead of working toward collaborative action

- an attitude of "I'm putting my time in" that reflects a lack of passion for and identification with the mission

Improving the health of an organization's culture is not an overnight process. After the new chief executive identifies the primary contributors to the imbalance, he or she can focus on creating a leadership platform that emphasizes the values, principles, and actions that must be embraced to strengthen organizational culture and function. A leadership platform is a powerful tool because it lays out the ground rules for healthier professional behaviors for staff and board and emphasizes positive expectations to be embraced by all.

Cultural dysfunction can occur under the watch of a seasoned chief executive as well, for many of the same reasons. A wise executive will keep close tabs on the balance of the organization's culture and implement similar actions and leadership messages to get the organization back on track to harmony and inclusiveness.

> *It really inspires confidence when the chief executive can help explain how the organization fits into the larger arena of competitors, partners, and other organizations.*

ESTABLISHING A LEARNING ORGANIZATION

One of the most important ways that a chief executive can inspire confidence and create a supportive environment is to make continuous learning part of the organization's culture, beginning with the personal pursuit of knowledge from the moment of arrival in the organization. Chief executives can expand their basic skills by reading professional journals, joining online forums, participating in conferences and workshops, interacting with peers and colleagues, and taking on new challenges that stretch their abilities.

Fundamentally, the board looks to the chief executive to be well informed about the field of interest that the nonprofit addresses, to know the latest developments, and to have recommendations for action if a change in course is needed. By surrounding themselves with advisors — including board and committee members, staff, and resource people from outside the organization — chief executives will find it easier to track changes in the field and will have a sounding board for testing possible responses.

Chief executives should be careful not to set themselves up as purveyors of all wisdom, however. In a culture of continuous learning, everyone should be expected to grow skills and abilities. The chief executive should share new information through newsletters, meetings, and electronic communication. He or she prepares others in the organization, especially board members, to be more knowledgeable about the cause, thus building confidence in the executive, themselves, and the organization as a whole.

One of the most important ways that a chief executive can inspire confidence and create a supportive environment is to make continuous learning part of the organization's culture.

The organization that uses the Board Member Expectations tool in Appendix 1 requires that board members "observe or participate in one [of the organization's] community service programs annually." This firsthand participation in the organization's mission delivery gives the board member not only a personal mission-related experience to share with potential volunteers and supporters, it also provides the board member with richer, experiential information from which to participate in board decision making around the organization's programs and services.

Professional development requires self-discipline because it is easy to be sidetracked by what needs to be done today, this week, or this year. A committed chief executive can use passion for the mission to nurture a curiosity to build knowledge. Envisioning the day that the organization conquers the problem it has set out to address can inspire the self-discipline that is necessary to continue learning and growing.

Ongoing environmental scanning is one of the most valuable services a chief executive can provide to the organization and the board.

MAINTAINING AN EXTERNAL FOCUS

Nonprofit organizations do not operate in a vacuum. In addition to understanding the organization and its cause, the chief executive should also be knowledgeable about the larger operating environment, including partners and competitors, funders, the organization's field of practice, and the nonprofit sector as a whole. Examining the programs and activities of other organizations, understanding proposed changes in government policy, and keeping abreast of general trends in funding or nonprofit sector accountability can yield valuable insights and help keep the organization and the board from being blindsided by unexpected changes in the operating environment.

Effective chief executives always have an eye on discovery in the external environment. They actively pursue new information and don't just passively react to what comes their way. They pose provocative questions to themselves and their boards, such as: What are the consequences of increased immigration on our programs? How will stock market trends affect our year-end giving? How will community support for our organization be affected by a scandal at a similar nonprofit? Many good organizations and programs have failed because the chief executive's head was buried deep in a pile of organization-related tasks without regard for the outside world.

Ongoing environmental scanning is one of the most valuable services a chief executive can provide to the organization and the board. Boards should make a habit of strategic thinking, and to do so they need the external perspective that helps them ask big-picture questions that drive their decisions about the organization's mission, priorities, and course of action. From the chief executive, they need both hard information and informed opinion, provided as part of ongoing give-and-take, not just in occasional reports.

Here's an example of one chief executive's approach to using external input to assist a board in its strategic thinking.

A board of a continuing care retirement community believed the offerings of its organization were excellent but knew that potential residents looked at a number of competitors to determine where to live. The chief executive helped arrange for a small group of board members to go on "field trips" to competitors to see their properties and learn from their successes and challenges. This experience helped the board members consider possible changes and better understand how others were approaching some of the same challenges they were facing.

Firsthand observations from participating board members shared with the balance of the board proved to be far more powerful than the comprehensive report that the Marketing Department had prepared the year before. This initiative reinforced the need to continue to explore what's new and different even when things are going well.

A savvy chief executive determines which sectors of the environment are most important to the organization and works through established networks of experts to collect and analyze information about current events in the targeted sectors. He or she may receive public policy information affecting the mission through a state or national association concerned with the cause. Mission-related developments in the field can be collected through interaction with colleagues inside and outside the organization, Really Simple Syndication (RSS) feeds, Google Alerts, Facebook cause and Fan page status updates, following organizations of interest on Twitter, and professional journals and newsletters. Many information sources send "breaking news" announcements that can be reviewed quickly and weighed for their impact.

Depending on the level of organizational impact and the urgency of the external information, the chief executive may choose to share it with selected board members or the full board. He or she may do so now, save the information for later, or discard it because it does not affect the organization. If another sector or group has primary leadership responsibility on the issue, the chief executive should check with external contacts to find out what action they may take and how the organization can be involved as a partner.

VIEW FROM THE BOARD CHAIR

Board members often don't know what they don't know. It really inspires confidence when the chief executive can help explain how the organization fits into the larger arena of competitors, partners, and other organizations. Board members don't deal with the organization's issues on a daily basis, and we may forget details that are important to the decision-making process. We look to the chief executive to provide key information that enables us to consider issues and give relevant input — including information about unknowns or uncertainties.

For the new chief executive, the challenges of getting to know the organization are generally straightforward. Gaining a clear understanding of the organization's past, its current goals and objectives, and the overall climate for the board's work are a few of the most critical areas. Board members usually are willing participants in getting the new chief executive up to speed. And when the predecessor has left the organization due to performance issues or differences in vision, it is imperative that the new chief executive be fully aware of the opportunities and areas of concern.

The more seasoned chief executive has different challenges to demonstrate the skill of knowing the organization. The board assumes the tenured individual is knowledgeable about all aspects of the organization, its needs, and the environment in which it operates. One might say the board doesn't know what the chief executive doesn't know! Some executives feel pressured to be the "answer man" when questions are posed. An executive who lacks information or confidence may react inappropriately, either shooting from the hip with questionable data or responding in a defensive manner. Neither approach works well over time. When chief executives welcome questions as a chance to learn something new, it gives us confidence that whatever knowledge is needed will be sought quickly and competently.

Another challenge for the experienced chief executive is balancing her understanding of the past without appearing to be stuck in the past. This perception can result when the chief executive dismisses a recommendation or stops pursuing a particular path because "we've tried this and it doesn't work." The chief executive must walk a fine line to prevent the board from making the same mistakes over and over while being open to the possibility that something is no longer a problem because the environment has changed. In either case, the board expects a chief executive to share prior approaches and challenges, offer perspectives on possible direction, and be open to thoughts and strategies offered — even when the new thought resembles previous attempts.

Knowledge of the organization is necessary for both the chief executive and the board, so helping to build the knowledge of board members is important. To assist the board to make informed decisions, balance the delivery of information by providing details supported by real life examples that reinforce the facts. Invite key staff members to present highlights of a program or service at board and committee meetings. Invite outside speakers who can present the external context and alternative approaches to stretch the thinking. The partnership of chief executive and board will be enhanced as everyone learns!

VIEW FROM THE CHIEF EXECUTIVE'S DESK

My first few years as chief executive were consumed with getting a handle on the mission, the finances, the board, and the community. Every minute of every day was an exciting and sometimes overwhelming learning experience as I soaked up knowledge and history that I could apply to the many demands at hand.

The board was an able partner captivated by the challenge of stabilizing the organization. Board members worked at a tireless pace, attending meetings, discussing finance and staff issues, acquiring new resources, and opening doors. They were great teachers who helped me get to know the community and build a new business plan. They knew the meaning of stability and gave their energy and contacts to help the organization achieve it.

After several intense years, we had the organizational foundation to do some serious planning and take some risks. I was growing impatient with the board. Board members came up with the silliest ideas, which often took the board and staff off track, and sometimes off mission. They became complacent about meeting attendance and less accountable for commitments they had made. Believing that everything was in good hands, they lost their sense of urgency. The staff did everything, and the board was along for the ride.

Then I had a wake-up call. I realized that change would have to begin with me. I needed to change my perception, my behavior, and the messages I was sending to the board. In my early years as chief executive, I looked to the board to teach me, but now it was both appropriate and necessary for me to teach the board. Setting the scene for thoughtful involvement of the full board in the strategic planning process was an important first step. The board learned right along with me, and all of us were better equipped to focus our vision for the future on an intentional path rather than react to scattered, sometimes off-track ideas just for the sake of generating activity.

The quality of board involvement definitely has changed for the better, and it is reflected in our board and committee meetings. We always make sure that each agenda includes one substantive discussion item with no easy or immediate answers. This gives board members a significant issue to tackle — not a report on how we currently do things or a request for feedback on how we can do better, but a challenge, either urgent or long-term, that we muster the courage to throw on the table and let board members discuss. The issue is framed with a set of provocative questions that tap the life and career experiences of board members.

One particularly provocative question was whether to dismiss board members for lack of financial giving at a certain minimum level. There were strong feelings on both sides. But the issue became less black-and-white when we considered individual situations, such as the board member who gave a $50 annual gift but opened doors to large government grants. This example led the board to think about alternatives for giving. In the end, it decided to use a holistic assessment of what each board member brings to the organization. While the board determined that each member would be expected to support the organization financially, the requirement was to be "within their own means at a meaningful level for them." The few board members who did not make financial contributions were referred to the nominating committee for a follow-up visit about their overall interest and commitment.

I am thankful for my wake-up call many years into my job as a chief executive. My sudden insight that I needed to shift from expecting the board to be the teacher to becoming the teacher myself came just in time. If it hadn't, I probably could have continued in my job, but I would have slighted the organization, its mission, and the gifts that the board could bring to the table.

PARTNERSHIP TIPS TO REMEMBER

- Have a strong grasp of your organization's field of interest, history, and business operation to inspire confidence in your partnership with the board.

- Continuously scan your external environment for challenges and opportunities important for the board's knowledge in doing its best work.

- Use the mission, vision, and core values to evaluate opportunities and challenges.

- Build your knowledge, which will inspire others to grow themselves.

- Tap the wisdom of long-time volunteer leaders and community partners to bring historical context to the story of the organization's journey through time and what defines its essence today.

- Use the strategic planning process as an opportunity to understand and/or refine your organization's culture and values.

- Establish and nurture a culture that sustains and grows the organization.

- Spot the signs of a dysfunctional culture and take speedy corrective action to bring balance and inclusiveness to the forefront of the board's work.

- Share mission-related knowledge with board members and encourage them to use it in governance decision-making and "pass it on" to their networks to enrich lives in the community.

- Surround yourself with advisors including board, committee members, staff, and outside resource people to track changes in your field and provide feedback about their impact to the organization.

- Include at least one provocative question at each board meeting that taps the life and career experiences of board members in addressing your organization's opportunities and challenges.

CHAPTER 3
CULTIVATE RELATIONSHIPS

Build habits and interactions that engage and involve the board.

Tending relationships involves attitudes and practices that must permeate the chief executive's whole approach to his or her position. Anyone who takes on the staff leadership of a nonprofit organization must be adept at cultivating relationships that enhance not only the chief executive's own effectiveness, but the board's potential for becoming an exceptional governing body that serves the organization's mission with vitality and commitment.

The most critical relationship, of course, is that of the chief executive and board chair. First, however, the chief executive must approach his or her job with flexibility, grace under pressure, and a positive and proactive attitude. With these pieces in place, he or she can nurture the all-important relationships that help engage, inspire, and energize board members. For the chief executive, cultivating relationships involves

1. practicing self-management

2. avoiding self-defeating habits

3. juggling roles and opportunities

4. creating and maintaining a partnership with the board chair

5. building relationships with individual board members

PRACTICING SELF-MANAGEMENT

Self-management can enhance the relationship between the chief executive and the board and yield benefits for the entire organization. Self-management means practicing the relationship behaviors that make oneself and others blossom. It means noticing these behaviors in others, admiring them, and reinforcing their continuance. And it means asking oneself from the very beginning: "What kind of relationship do I want and how do I sustain it?"

> *The chief executive who gives the board member full and active attention is the chief executive who knows the value of building productive relationships.*

It can be a challenge to balance what is human nature with what is needed in a leader. There may be times when the chief executive morphs into other life forms while interacting with others. Making a list of these behavioral pitfalls is a helpful exercise. The chief executive may bark at the board chair who calls in midthought with a request or new idea, growl at the staff member who complains about a committee chair's lack of follow-up, or take on the qualities of a robot while moving through a project or conversation step by step, according to the plan, without regard to the value of new information.

When the chief executive recognizes that personal behavior might be sending a message that he or she has become something other than a leader, it's time to reel back in and take control. A first step in self-management is reflecting on her list of personal pitfalls. Are some of them particularly troublesome and repetitive? Did new pitfalls emerge that she had control over in the past? The executive may ask, "What led to my stressful behavior?" "What did I learn from falling off the wagon?" "How can I be more aware of the warning signs when I am allowing my buttons to be pushed?" "Would outside help from a friend, colleague, or leadership coach be useful?"

This is also a good time to review, recommit, and practice basic tenets of self-management:

1. **Stay organized.** A world of chaos can lead to chaotic behavior. Organize information for easy access. Keep a calendar handy and don't overschedule, leaving no time for the unexpected (which can always be expected) or for thought and reflection. A good chief executive also maintains an uncluttered mind, taking the time to record appointments, phone numbers, ideas, and prospective contacts and filing them in a workable system. This way there is space in the executive's head to welcome the wisdom the board has to offer.

2. **Ask questions.** Remember the wonder the world held when we were in our youth? How did the world begin? Do clouds have babies? These rich questions challenged the wisdom of our parents. Our job journey and our life journey are to gain wisdom through our experiences and the experiences of others. The chief executive who fails to ask rich questions that tap the wisdom of the board will fail to bring the value to the organization that he or she is charged with delivering as a leader. To help better understand how to frame questions that challenge thinking and get the board engaged, see Appendix 2: Catalytic Questions.

3. **Listen.** The chief executive who gives the board member full and active attention is the chief executive who knows the value of building productive relationships. Interrupting, checking a mobile device, or answering the telephone are signs that a chief executive is distracted and lacks the self-control to seize the moment and the value it offers.

4. **Concentrate.** The board expects that a good deal of the value the chief executive brings to the organization is experience and wisdom. The whirling dervish who never takes time to consider the ever-changing pieces of the puzzle may show value as a hard worker, but not as a change agent. While there are many demands on the chief executive's attention, it's essential to make a space to examine the pieces of the puzzle, try new fits, and make new discoveries that inspire deeper and more meaningful action. To set the stage for reflection and concentration, some chief executives find a quiet space at the library or a coffee shop near the office, turn off their cell phones during long car trips, post a "meeting in progress" sign on their office doors, or engage an impartial outside advisor in a rousing discussion to gain insight and focus.

5. **Be flexible.** Seasoned chief executives know that flexibility and adaptability are important attributes in determining the balance of leadership that the organization needs. The chief executive who must control everything is risking constant stress, disappointment, and failure. Having control may seem to offer some sense of security and comfort. But the board expects the organization to grow and prosper and its chief executive to remain proactively engaged as they embark for uncharted territory, unknown parts, or even a familiar path that didn't lead to success in the past. A chief executive without the courage and foresight to take this journey with the board is doing the organization a disservice.

6. **Seek feedback.** It's not enough to just be open to others when they have differing opinions. A successful chief executive will deliberately ask for input about activities, about their own performance and other challenges the organization is facing. And to gain the most value of this effort, a chief executive doesn't just request this of those who generally agree with her, she also looks to those who typically take opposing views. By doing so, the chief executive will have a better sense of potential issues that most likely would be raised in the future — with a chance to address them right away.

7. **Build a support network.** Seek out mentors and informal groups or professional associations of chief executives who can be called on for honest feedback, to serve as a sounding board, and be helpful in determining approaches for dealing with challenges or opportunities.

8. **Be your own devil's advocate.** Consider alternative approaches when proposing a course of action. Would other ways work better? Wise chief executives think about the potential for unintended consequences of their strategies and actions. Could someone misinterpret what I'm trying to do? Are there ways to approach a problem that could yield greater success…or have fewer negative outcomes? Thinking through a situation from different perspectives can enhance problem-solving and decision-making skills. And by doing so, you are able to anticipate questions, prepare for opposing views, and generally enhance your initial proposal.

9. **Be open and approachable.** Board members can give their best when they know what they offer will be welcomed and seriously considered.

10. **Diffuse anger and conflict.** Respect different opinions without judging, and if necessary, defer emotionally charged issues to a later time. These efforts can go a long way in keeping relationships on track.

11. **Learn how to "read" people.** Exercising empathy is a way of putting yourself in someone else's shoes and hearing the message as they might hear it, feeling the delivery as they might feel it, and drawing conclusions about the outcome of the interaction as they might see it as well. With successful communication as the ultimate goal, the wise chief executive will become a skilled empathizer.

The chief executive has made an important first step in self-management when he or she recognizes a personal discomfort with surrendering control and the resulting negative impact on the organization. Exercising behaviors that demonstrate flexibility are the next step toward building the strength of this important skill:

- Delegate projects to others.

- Allow board members to work on tasks without hovering; if you don't give them some freedom to operate, they may wonder why you asked for their involvement.

- Pick your battles.

- Look for the positive first.

- Don't sweat the small stuff when something does not go as planned.

- Work with the board chair to frame ventures into uncharted territories that break the journey into smaller steps or projects that provide opportunities to check in and chart progress.

- Don't put the brakes on just because you are uncomfortable.

AVOIDING SELF-DEFEATING HABITS

Chief executives are busy people doing a difficult job. As human beings in a high-stress situation, they are also subject to temptations that can limit their own professional and personal development as well as the effectiveness of the board. Ten tips to avoid bad habits that every chief executive should heed are

1. **Don't do everything yourself.** Let's face it: There's much truth in the adage, "If you want something done right, do it yourself." And sometimes the amount of time required supporting board member volunteers in key tasks — such as donor cultivation and solicitation, board member recruitment, or legislative testimony — creates the temptation for executives to fly solo. Board members are sometimes grateful to get off the hook, confident that the task is in skilled hands. The chief executive who is a one-person band will work long, lonely hours while the organization's volunteer leaders fail to develop the skills they need to help lighten the executive's load. He or she must learn to share

leadership, and invest in supporting and developing board leaders even when it feels like there's no time. The investment will produce dividends for years to come.

2. **Don't blame the staff.** When things go poorly and the chief executive needs to offer an explanation to the board, it can be tempting to blame subordinates for failure — especially if they are in fact responsible. But keep in mind that the chief executive is responsible for hiring decisions and for managing employees. Bringing performance issues before the board, even indirectly, makes the chief executive look like an ineffective manager and invites board intrusion. Where staff actions and performance are concerned, the buck stops with the chief executive, who must take responsibility for the staff members, manage them, and accept responsibility for their performance when dealing with the board.

3. **Don't hide behind the board.** For the chief executive faced with difficult decisions, the board can serve as a convenient scapegoat. "I'd like to give larger raises, but the board limited us to 3 percent this year," or "I support your program but the board voted to cut it," may seem like appealing alternatives to assuming direct ownership of an unpopular action. This strategy has significant pitfalls, however. It reduces the staff's confidence in the chief executive by creating the impression that the board often overrides or ignores the executive's recommendations. It invites staff members to become freelance lobbyists with individual board members around issues, decisions, or programs that they care about. And it undermines the executive's integrity and the organization's transparency. The board of directors should not be a mysterious black box for staff. With a few exceptions, senior staff should be able to observe board meetings and board decisions, and chief executives should take full ownership of their decisions and recommendations.

4. **Don't drown the board in information.** No chief executive ever wants to be criticized by the board for failing to share a significant piece of information, yet it's sometimes challenging to know what is most significant or what information may come back to haunt the executive later. That may be one reason why most executives err on the side of providing too much information to board members. Too much information also has a soporific effect on boards — it keeps them quiet and a little groggy. The chief executive's job is to keep board members awake, not lull them to sleep; to point out three or four needles, and not dump the entire haystack on the board table. (See Chapter 4 for more guidance on informing and communicating.)

5. **Don't leave well enough alone.** Many chief executives are so grateful that they have a good board — or even an OK board — that they are extremely reluctant to change the status quo. The somewhat effective board that causes no harm and doesn't require much care or maintenance may seem preferable to an unknown alternative, or to the extremely engaged board that needs extensive support, creates new work for the chief executive, and has its own ideas about mission and direction. Chief executives should keep in mind that their primary responsibility is to tap all available resources to produce the best outcomes for the organization and its mission, not to preserve their position or make their own life easier.

6. **Don't cry wolf.** Every now and then, a chief executive will be tempted to spur a sleepy board into action by crying wolf — declaring that immediate board action is required to forestall imminent disaster. This scenario most often occurs around fundraising: "If we can't raise $10,000 by next week we won't be able to make payroll, or we'll need to shut down a major program." Another example is the chief executive who threatens to resign every few months. Whatever the situation, chief executives should think carefully before crying wolf. The chief executive who raises an urgent problem, then pulls a rabbit out of a hat to fix things when the board fails to take action, will gradually convince board members that he or she is an alarmist and that things will always work out in the end without their intervention. And the chief executive who threatens to quit should be prepared to follow through when the board eventually accepts the resignation.

7. **Don't focus on a few board members and ignore the rest.** On many boards, a few key members do most of the work, and most chief executives are likely to enjoy working with some board members more than others. For those reasons and others, cliques or tiers of power often develop on boards. Chief executives who focus their interactions on board officers and a few key friends can usually get most of the outcomes they're looking for — the board accepts their recommendations, makes the right decisions, and even gives them positive feedback about performance. What's more, building relationships with a few key people takes much less time than interacting regularly with 15 or 20 people. The problem is other board members notice. If their participation isn't meaningful, they will participate less. If the board is dominated by an inside circle, those on the outside will lose interest and become more dissatisfied. Every board member is an important asset to the organization and should be cultivated and developed. A board in which all members contribute is more likely to govern well than a board that is dominated by a few friends of the chief executive.

8. **Don't avoid uncomfortable situations.** When a board member is issuing task directives to a staff member, there is enough discomfort to go around. The chief executive feels bypassed. The staff member feels overwhelmed and unsure who is calling the shots. And, the board member probably is just as frustrated that he feels he has to take responsibility for the details. Or, maybe it's just a board member on a power trip who enjoys having others do his bidding. Whatever the case, a frank discussion with the board member at the first sign of trouble is in order. Developing clear expectations for staff and the board member in regard to the particular project can go a long way in alleviating the stress of the situation.

9. **Don't avoid sharing bad news at the first smell of trouble.** Sharing bad news is rarely a positive experience, but when the chief executive keeps bad news to him- or herself, there is no good outcome for any involved. He or she may be hoping the tides will change and the situation will dissipate, sparing the board of any negative consequences. Or, the chief executive may feel personal responsibility for the bad turn of events and be embarrassed, even fearful of exposing his or her shortcomings. Depending on the situation, leaving bad news to fend for itself can put the board and the organization at risk of financial distress, litigation, failure of necessary programming, and erosion of credibility, just to name a few.

10. **Don't get too personal with board members.** While there are certainly board members that the chief executive just clicks with because of complementary personalities or shared interests, these familiar connections do not have a place in the boardroom or in any of the organization's work. For the board as a group to do its work effectively, each member must feel that the chief executive and board chair have an equal connection to them, not tainted by personal feelings or preferences. Board members who feel "left out" or on unequal footing are not able to feel secure in giving their best ideas and talents to the important task of governing the organization.

JUGGLING ROLES AND OPPORTUNITIES

Seasoned chief executives know that anyone who expects a typical day to go according to plan is in for an awakening. It's nearly impossible to make a to-do list and leave the office at the end of the day having checked off most or all of the items. Most of the chief executive's work is done as an agent of the board, and its needs, requirements, and strategic direction must be considered with every action.

When successful, the chief executive's juggling act enables him or her to size up situations quickly and determine the appropriate roles for the executive, the board chair, and the full board. The executive must also recognize new opportunities as they present themselves, weigh their value to the organization, and reprioritize tasks and resources to address current situations and opportunities. Chief executives can't be irritated or frustrated by the rate of change that they must deal with; otherwise, their energy will be sapped and they won't be able to reach out in an inviting way to seek the help and support of board members in navigating the ship through ever-choppy waters.

The role chief executives play can change with the situation, the issue, the time of year, the skills of the board chair, and the collective composition of the board. It may be necessary to select from the many hats on the executive's hat rack to assume a needed role for a particular situation. If a visible community leader who opened doors for the organization to participate in major community forums rotates off the board, the chief executive needs to plan for a decrease in community visibility, the replacement of this board member with another who has the same abilities, or an increase in the executive's own personal public appearances. Or the board might lose a strong development committee chair that had real skill and tenacity when it came to holding the board's feet to the fire regarding annual giving. The new chair might have great access to major gifts but less comfort in dogging his or her peers for an annual contribution. This scenario might give the chief executive a bit of relief in pursuing prospective major donors while requiring more effort in developing board giving.

GROWING BOARD MEMBERS

The chief executive needs to know how to compensate when board skills aren't enough to accomplish a task, and how to develop board members' aptitudes. A board member who takes on a new position may need time to grow into the responsibilities. The chief executive can work with the board member on specific tasks, attend meetings, and be prepared to coach or train when necessary. Building board members' confidence is another way chief executives support the board. Some board members, for example, may not be experienced at representing the organization in front of large groups or the media. The chief executive can help a board member ease into public presentations by inviting him or her to make a committee report at a board meeting, to acknowledge sponsors and other board members at a special event, or to introduce guest speakers at a workshop. With each experience, the board member's confidence grows and prepares him or her to assume future leadership requirements with more comfort and success.

Most of the chief executive's work is done as an agent of the board, and its needs, requirements, and strategic direction must be considered with every action.

The chief executive also needs to be adept at spotting board members who will take well to learning skills and assuming leadership roles. The board member who comes to meetings prepared, asks questions at meetings and in between meetings, or just asks what more he or she can do is a prime candidate for leadership development. An astute chief executive keeps these board members in mind when there are issues to research, a task force to lead, or a program or service to observe and evaluate. The chief executive exposes these "diamonds in the rough" to rich experiences that will add to their understanding of the organization, deepen their commitment, and prepare them to assume greater leadership roles.

Board members can give their best when they know what they offer will be welcomed and seriously considered.

BOARD RELATIONSHIPS

The chief executive's most important relationship is with the board chair. The two leaders are interdependent. They swim or sink together. Their interactions are watched and evaluated by other board members and staff. A positive, constructive partnership signals direction, purpose, and excitement about the organization's mission, while a lackluster or confrontational relationship will have a detrimental effect on the board and on individual members' commitment.

BUILDING FROM THE GROUND UP

When conditions are right, the relationship begins long before the chair takes the job. Organizations should have a process — and many do — through which board members progress to the position of board chair. The board chair should have experience with the organization and a track record of working successfully with the chief executive on a variety of projects and issues. A board chair can increase his or her success by serving as chair-elect for one or more years, preparing for the position, shadowing the current board chair, and being included in strategic discussions that cut across a variety of issues and topics of importance to the organization.

With this foundation, a chief executive has an excellent platform upon which to build the leadership partnership. Early on, the two leaders should establish their expectations of each other in areas such as communication style and values, frequency of reporting and meetings, functions in which the board chair is expected to participate, and shared and individual priorities. The chief executive may encourage the new board chair to adopt a platform for his or her term, similar in concept to the platforms adopted by candidates for political office. The platform should reflect the organization's strategic goals and the unique interests and skills that the board chair can offer (see Appendix 3 for a sample board chair platform).

Increased interaction with the incoming chair will also give the chief executive the information and experience needed to create a successful partnership. Often the new chair is a committee chair or a key committee member. The chief executive should make a point of attending meetings in which the chair-elect is involved and observe him or her in action. In this way, the executive can take stock of strengths and weaknesses and provide opportunities to enhance leadership skills. This observation process will also alert the chief executive to skills he or she may need to develop to complement the new chair. Veteran chief executives know that flexibility and adaptability are important attributes in determining the balance of leadership that the organization needs.

Before the board chair takes office, the chief executive should suggest a discussion about expectations. Aside from reviewing their formal job descriptions, the two leaders may want to craft a communications and accountability pact. This agreement can cover issues ranging from honest feedback about the chief executive's performance to a schedule of weekly telephone calls or monthly in-person meetings (see Appendix 4 for a sample pact).

In a recently formed organization that has not yet established a "career path" for the role of the board chair, the chief executive should help the governance committee select a candidate who has previous experience in nonprofit governance. The executive should take particular care in providing opportunities for the new board chair to interact with board members (to build the team), with colleagues in the field (to build knowledge of the external environment), and with customers that the organization serves (to build the passion).

If the Road Gets Rocky

A board chair who has lost his or her way can cause conflict in the organization and in his or her partnership with the chief executive. The chief executive must keep the lines of communication open when the partnership seems to be taking two different paths. The chief executive needs to define exactly what the conflict is and how it creates a problem. This information should be shared as tactfully and gently as possible. The goal is to work toward collaboration to find a solution. Partnership is not about the strongest force winning. It is about learning from each other and understanding that combined wisdom can be even stronger than the wisdom of one.

> *Veteran chief executives know that flexibility and adaptability are important attributes in determining the balance of leadership that the organization needs.*

RELATIONSHIPS WITH INDIVIDUAL BOARD MEMBERS

Although the board makes decisions as a group, it is made up of individuals who are each accountable for taking fiduciary responsibility and fulfilling their duties of care, loyalty, and obedience. The chief executive who sees the board only as a group is missing out on the value that he or she can derive — personally, professionally, and organizationally — by developing relationships with individual board members.

Most board members appreciate a chief executive who enjoys a relationship with them independent of the full board relationship. Such interactions allow the chief executive to build the board member's passion and commitment and invite the board member to share life lessons and insights that may not come to light in a formal group setting.

Just as pearls are found by diving deep and checking many oysters, the chief executive who takes the time for individual relationships with board members will discover many valuable connections for the organization.

Some chief executives set personal goals for the number of interactions per week or per day with board members. One chief executive joined a local leadership club that offered an educational lunch and featured speakers every month. With the opportunity to bring guests to each luncheon, she invited one or two board members to join her each month for exposure to a timely topic and time to visit and bond. Without a goal to engage with board members individually, it is easy to be swallowed up by management issues and miss the opportunity to further develop the organization's greatest resource — its board.

Just like everyone else, chief executives need a sounding board to help them sort out struggles in life. But it's important to remember that people don't sign on to the board to become the chief executive's personal support system. Some board members may take an interest in the chief executive's personal and professional development, offer thoughtful feedback, and share information about themselves. The chief executive should always be cautious with these personal relationships, since board members form their perceptions based on both personal and professional skills and weaknesses. When socializing with board members, the chief executive should take care to present a positive image that reflects well upon his or her performance on behalf of the organization. There are many places a nonprofit chief executive can let his or her hair down. Generally, in the company of board members is not one of them.

WE'RE ALL ONLY HUMAN

In all the interpersonal relationships that come into play in a nonprofit organization, it's important to remember that at the end of the day, we're all only human. Inevitably there will be missteps, overlooked opportunities, and less-than-perfect decisions. Leading an organization is a great honor and responsibility. If the chief executive or board chair allows the weight of the responsibility to dictate an environment of flawlessness, the board may be driven to a place where members don't participate and are afraid to speak up. People know they are only human, and if perfection is expected, they are sure to fail — so they just don't try. The organizational culture will deteriorate into scapegoating, blame, lack of action, and low morale.

Partnership is not about the strongest force winning. It is about learning from each other and understanding that combined wisdom can be even stronger than the wisdom of one.

On the flip side, there are many daily reminders for the chief executive that the world isn't a perfect place. When he or she recognizes flaws in the relationship with the board chair or board members, or among members of the board, it is time to take immediate action. Situations that require remediation might include a board chair and chief executive with conflicting visions for the organization. Or the board chair may be totally off base, leading the board without regard to mission or strategic plan. Sometimes, for reasons beyond anyone's control — illness, a job change, a move — a board chair position may turn over several times in a short period, leaving the chief executive and board to plug holes instead of move forward. It is also not unusual to have at least one board member who is high-maintenance, hostile, or doesn't play well with others, including the chief executive.

When the chief executive recognizes these symptoms or situations, he or she can direct change through personal behavior. The executive can disarm the perfect board chair by sharing his or her own struggles, mistakes, and missed opportunities. By seeking feedback and sharing lessons from a less-than-perfect experience, the chief executive can lead the board chair to be candid about his or her own learning experiences. It helps to be direct, asking: "What are some learning experiences you've had that have made a difference in your success?" Openness and honesty can be the first step in changing the culture of perfection into one that appreciates people for their commitment, courage, and willingness to take risks to serve the mission.

By maintaining close relationships with at least a few tenured members of the board, the chief executive will have someone who can assess, advise, and/or assist with sticky situations that arise in a board chair partnership that has gone off track. Of course, the chief executive should respect the relationship and turn to outside assistance only in an impasse. Venting everyday concerns with other board members is dangerous territory. Tenured board members may also be helpful in providing at least temporary leadership if the board chair position has been vacated unexpectedly while a search is under way for a replacement.

VIEW FROM THE BOARD CHAIR

The relationship between chief executive and board chair is a unique partnership. Each relies on the other to perform his or her role successfully. The two must be willing to blend their styles and approaches to leadership to produce a cohesive environment conducive to active involvement of the board and staff. There needs to be a strong understanding of our respective roles and responsibilities. If one of us is less experienced, the more seasoned person must find ways to help the other develop skills and abilities quickly.

The most effective boards are graced with skillful leaders in the chief executive and the board chair. Both should be effective communicators, and ideally both are viewed as equally open to feedback from board and staff. Through careful agenda development and meeting planning, the chief executive and board chair will convey a shared focus.

Close, working friendships often develop, but we as board chairs need to remain independent enough to evaluate the chief executive's performance and to respond to board members who express issues or concerns. Balancing a friendly, effective relationship with frank and open communication requires a strong chair and a willing chief executive who welcomes feedback.

I have served on some boards where the relationship between these two leaders is energizing and on others where the atmosphere is tense and argumentative. Both leaders share the responsibility to develop an effective relationship. When the chief executive experiences problems, the best course of action is to identify areas of difference. How does the board chair prefer to communicate? Does the current job description adequately reflect the chair's view of what the chief executive should be doing? Does the board chair support the strategic plan or believe it needs revision?

To aid in the resolution of serious relationship issues, there are interpersonal skills techniques that the chief executive should develop. By applying such skills to situations where there is friction between the two leaders, the problems will be addressed as organizational issues rather than personal attacks.

- Demonstrate your own openness and approachability so the individual will be willing to have an honest discussion about differences in vision, strategies, and whatever else is being disputed. Keep the focus on your desire to understand the individual's point of view.

- Diffuse anger and conflict by focusing the discussion toward efforts to clarify and resolve differences. Ask clarifying questions such as: "Help me understand what you'd like me to do" and "What's one thing you would like me to do differently?"

- Learn how to read people. People are all different and identifying what motivates them, what their goals are, and how they define success all help the chief executive understand how to work more effectively. Frame your suggestions based on how your "audience" will receive the message. Behavioral psychology sections in bookstores are good places to look for resources to help develop "people reading" skills. BoardSource's toolkit *Boardroom Chemistry: Getting Your Board to Govern as a Team* also offers insight on how successful boards have figured out how to make the most of the various relationships (chief executive to board, board chair to board, and board member to board member) so that the work of the board assumes greater importance than any individual or relationship.

- Use the strategic plan to help evaluate whether the issue is critical, nice but not necessary, or really not germane to the goals and objectives of the organization. Sometimes issues are the result of differing opinions about what should be the focus of the organization. Until this is resolved, the tension will remain.

Once the concerns are fully discussed, both leaders should have a common understanding of how best to fulfill the mission of the organization together. After all, that's what should be the driving force for all their actions.

VIEW FROM THE CHIEF EXECUTIVE'S DESK

When I first took a job as a chief executive, I was not certain that my level of maturity and experience was up to the task. I was somewhat astounded that I was selected for such a responsible position having never held a chief executive job before. I felt the weight of the world on my shoulders as I anticipated trying to live up to the organization's trust and expectations.

I set out to produce far more than the small organization was capable of and expected a far higher level of achievement than it was prepared to produce. I obsessed over every move to avoid a misstep or a failure. I believed that the board trusted me to do the right thing, and I was going to push myself into a froth to figure out what the right thing was, if I didn't already know — and there was a lot more I didn't know than I did know. I had also inherited an $80,000 deficit and no money in the bank.

The staff thought I was crazy. They complained of micromanagement, and some headed for the hills, only adding to the stress. I developed an ulcer at age 30. Luckily, the board chair was a wise individual, experienced in the game of life. She told me that the board recognized my raw talent and my desire to make a difference. She shared that the board was in there for the long haul to work with me to bring the organization back to stability and then to growth. She reminded me that my role was to work with her to tap every treasure the board had to offer and provide the structure and support to board members to help put their treasures to work to benefit the mission. She provided the perspective I needed to invite her and members of the board to share ownership for the organization and stop thinking I should save the world alone. She reinforced that I was chosen for the position because I was 100 percent genuine. I knew myself, accepted who I was, and had a hunger to improve.

What a relief! I accepted that it was OK for me to be "just human," and that might just be the best part of me. Understanding that the board had to be a partner in my work as a chief executive was a wonderful gift that this board chair gave me. She worked with me to develop a list of immediate needs, organize meetings with board members to invite their participation and resources in stabilizing the organization, and inspire board members to take an active role in getting us back on track. She made board members feel confident that the organization was going places and convinced them that they needed to recruit new board and committee members to enjoy the success ahead. Within one year, our finances were stable, committees with fresh new leadership were in place, and non-doer board members were replaced by active participants eager to join the cause.

Many new chief executives or seasoned executives who get off track may not be so fortunate. But we all can recognize when we're trying to be superhuman. Our heart races, we are impatient with others, and we toss and turn at night. We believe that no one can do it as well as we can. We have the weight of the world on our shoulders, and there's no one in sight to relieve us. When we recognize these signs, it is important to take care of ourselves, embrace our humanness and that of others, quiet our minds, organize our world, and reach out to others to share the struggle and the load. The chief executive and board need each other, working in partnership to be successful and to enjoy the life-enriching benefits that come from doing this important work.

PARTNERSHIP TIPS TO REMEMBER

- Work with and through others to achieve desired outcomes — the saying "It takes a village" does apply!

- Make a list of your behavioral pitfalls so that you can recognize the triggers and nip the bad behaviors in the bud.

- Maintain polish and professionalism by staying organized, talking less and listening more, taking time to concentrate and remaining flexible.

- Don't be trapped by self-defeating behaviors that rob you of putting your best foot forward with the board — doing everything yourself, blaming the staff for mistakes, avoiding responsibility for your decisions, and resting on your laurels to the detriment of the development of the board and staff.

- Continuously forecast the impact of today's challenges and opportunities out into the future to provide the board a variety of scenarios and outcomes to consider as they deliberate action.

- Be responsive to the skills and experiences of the board chair and adjust your focus and approach to match the unmet needs of the organization.

- Spot board members who will take well to learning new skills and assuming leadership. Expose them to opportunities to test and grow their skills.

- Look for talent among board members and nurture potential leaders to build their skills and experiences by giving them opportunities to chair a committee or workgroup, make presentations on behalf of the organization, and participate in a fundraising call to a potential donor.

- Know that every board member has value to offer and discover how to best maximize what each has to offer.

- Remember your relationship with the board chair is interdependent. Positive or negative, it sets the tone for the relationships among other board members and staff.

- Begin to develop your relationship with the board chair long before he assumes the role through collaborative work inside the organization and by representing the organization at community events and workshops as a team.

- Admit your mistakes and shortcomings to the board and staff. No one is perfect. Honesty and thoughtfulness about improvements that can be made put others at ease to forge ahead and avoid the inertia that a perfectionist goal often creates.

CHAPTER 4
INFORM AND COMMUNICATE

Prepare board members for success.

Chief executives who treat knowledge as a critical intellectual asset are preparing their boards for success. As they inform and communicate with their boards with consistency and creativity, they are practicing their own form of what's known as knowledge management: the ongoing practice of gathering high-quality information from inside and outside the organization, putting it in order according to a practical system, and using it to support and enhance the organization's work and its chances of success. Even though a chief executive has a great deal of information to sift through every day, developing the discipline of careful sifting, thought, and sharing will have positive payoffs. Board members will be in the loop, equipped to speak confidently about the organization, and prepared to act when needed.

The chief executive is expected to be the chief "hunter and gatherer" of information, but hunting and gathering are only the beginning. Selecting information to help the board make decisions in the best interest of the organization takes conscientious effort, a solid system of organization, and enough empathy to determine what information board members need, how they need it, and when they need it.

Information in and of itself is not communication. Communication is the magic that happens in the process of exchanging information and ideas. Chief executives should not underestimate the importance of their communications skills and behaviors. Many well-informed, well-educated chief executives have failed as leaders because they couldn't activate the magic of effective communication.

INFORMATION IS EVERYTHING

Knowing when, where, how, and how much to communicate can make a big difference in the chief executive's capacity to partner effectively with the board. E-mail and social networking place an overwhelming amount of information at our fingertips. Every day chief executives are deluged with information from staff, board members, and stakeholders. The mail and online sources bring new business publications, breaking news, and professional journals.

A Web search can produce thousands of references on any topic in a few seconds. Under this bombardment, the challenge in looking for strategic information is to be the hunter rather than the passive recipient.

Part of hunting and gathering happens within the organization, as the chief executive keeps abreast of what is happening in order to document progress toward goals, highlight lessons learned, and reveal challenges before they become problems. Information about program effectiveness gleaned from evaluation, for example, is indispensable for the board in making decisions about future directions.

But information originating exclusively from internal sources must be complemented by information on the external environment. Competition, new discoveries in the field, changes in government policy, and the positions and plans of partnerships and coalitions are all important to the organization. If the chief executive is not using personal relationships with individuals and groups outside the organization to hunt for information, he or she has incomplete knowledge with which to consider actions and help the board make the best decisions.

Hunting for information outside the organization might include

- joining professional organizations with a connection to the organization's field of interest, nonprofit management, or public policy

- participating in coalitions of organizations with common interests

- attending community events that offer networking with colleagues, supporters, and funders

- reaching out to experts on topics of interest

- participating in workshops or seminars to hone personal knowledge and understanding

- joining social networking cause and fan groups or following similar causes on Twitter

- crowdsourcing requests for information/possible solutions through social networking sites (*crowdsourcing* is the act of outsourcing tasks typically performed inside the organization to a large group or community through an open call)

The gathering process — selecting information of value and storing it where it can be easily found and accessed — goes hand in hand with hunting. Every organization needs its own system for managing information. A simple first step is to separate information that can be used now from information that may be used later.

The chief executive should be familiar with the organization's information repositories and manage his or her own repositories. With the challenges of small staffs, frequent employee turnover, and the lack of highly sophisticated technology, the chief executive may reach a standstill if he or she has depended on others to organize critical information. If there is no paid staff, the chief executive has the daunting responsibility of keeping up to date independently.

EVALUATING INFORMATION TO SUPPORT THE BOARD

Hunting and gathering information is all fine and well (and necessary), but it means little if the information is not shared with the right people, at the right time, and in the best format. Chief executives need to balance the time they invest in gaining knowledge with the time needed to make it useful to themselves and others. Getting into this habit can be difficult, especially when the chief executive feels more comfortable in one area or the other. Either extreme — abundance or scarcity of information — can create pitfalls for chief executives and their boards.

Knowing when, where, how, and how much to communicate can make a big difference in the chief executive's capacity to partner effectively with the board.

Most time-management experts advise dealing with each piece of paper, e-mail, or text message only once. Otherwise, the breadth of what has been collected soon will be impossible to tackle. Good chief executives constantly evaluate information that could help the board do its job in order to determine what should be shared with all or some members of the board, when, and how.

The chief executive must share certain essential information that provides the foundation for a responsible board, including information about the board's obligations, meeting dates, agendas, and meeting minutes. But preparing board members for exceptional performance requires information that goes beyond the nuts and bolts of board service. They need information that

- adds to their knowledge of the organization's mission or field of interest

- deals with a current organizational issue or challenge that will likely need board deliberation and action now or in the future

- pertains to changes or advances outside the organization that may affect it now or in the future and alerts them to potential risks, such as a disgruntled employee or volunteer, a poor outcome on an audit, unstable finances, the potential loss of a major source of revenue, or a competitor that is not willing to coexist peacefully

Some chief executives have found it useful to share "the things that keep them up at night" with the board or at least the board chair. The most successful confessions focus on longer-term, big-picture items like organizational dependence on one major donor or a compromised relationship with a key partner in the field rather than day-to-day management issues like a key staff position being vacant. This type of information can help a board understand where the chief executive's "head is at" and offer feedback, resources, and support. It also provides important insight into the context upon which the chief executive has set her priorities and action on behalf of the business operation of the organization.

Chief executives need to balance the time they invest in gaining knowledge with the time needed to make it useful to themselves and others.

GETTING THE RIGHT INFORMATION TO THE RIGHT PEOPLE

In the days when communicating with board members required stuffing and addressing 30 envelopes or making 30 phone calls, chief executives put a bit more thought and consideration into getting the right information to the board members who needed it. Although they may be tempted by the ease and immediacy of e-mail to include "the world," chief executives need to avoid indiscriminately blasting every interesting bit of news to every board member. While doing so may take a task off the chief executive's to-do list, it will also irritate busy board members and condition them to ignore the information.

Obviously, all board members need to receive meeting notices, minutes, newsletters and news releases, invitations to special events, periodic financial statements, some public policy updates, and information about notable personal or professional events involving board and staff. For information that falls outside that framework, chief executives should be thoughtful about targeting recipients.

The board chair will generally expect more frequent and detailed information than other board members. The board chair is the key partner to the chief executive in determining the development of the board agenda and meeting flow, so frequent contact is inherent in the role. This individual can also help the chief executive determine what information needs to go to all board members, some board members, or to no one. Keeping the board chair up to date on potentially sensitive issues ensures they are prepared to respond as needed.

Other board officers and committee chairs may expect more frequent contact with the chief executive or key staff contacts regarding information that affects their officer role or their committee's work. Many chief executives also have informal groupings of board members who can help analyze information and provide solid advice on particular topics.

THE BEAUTY OF COMMUNICATION

Communication is far more than transmitting information. The chief executive's communication style and behavior make the difference between information that falls flat and useful facts, ideas, and options that engage board members and give them energy and confidence. In this era of e-mail, blogging, texting, and social networking, it is worth remembering that information may be transmitted electronically or on paper, but meaningful communication happens in person. As chief executives communicate with board members, they should keep in mind the following tips:

- **Pay attention to nonverbal cues.** Up to 75 percent of communication is nonverbal and transferred through body language. Eye-rolling or checking text messages during a meeting sends the message, "You irritate me" or "What you are discussing is not important." Board members do not have the advantage of interacting every day with the chief executive, and their opinions are shaped by the isolated instances when they see him or her in action.

- **Be honest and open.** The chief executive should always provide accurate information about what the truth is at the time. Painting an overly optimistic picture and selling it as current fact is counterproductive. Even with every good intention, situations do not always turn out as hoped. Chief executives who present smoke and mirrors as reality will eventually be viewed as unreliable and untrustworthy. Boards infinitely prefer good surprises — times when things go better than expected after the executive has presented a realistic assessment of the situation — to the eventual collapse of unrealistic expectations. Honesty and openness applies to the good news as well as the bad. The board wants to share in the organization's successes and be reminded of the pivotal role it plays. A chief executive who only shares bad news makes a board burn out quickly, since it will tend to operate at a high level of stress with little reward.

- **Deal with issues head on.** Don't let things sit. When certain information, like a cash crunch, may pose a risk to the organization, it is dangerous for the chief executive to let it simmer in the hope that he or she can take care of the situation without involving the board. The chief executive may want to spare the board the stress, or he or she may feel responsible for the problem and want to preserve credibility. Invariably, these kinds of issues do not go away, and they may even be serious enough to threaten the long-term viability of the organization.

- **If you don't know, say so.** The best tool for the chief executive to use when information is unknown or unavailable is the response, "I don't know, but I'll find out." Pretending to have the correct information and passing it along to the board to preserve ego or avoid embarrassment creates a risk for the organization and a sense among the board that the chief executive is untrustworthy or inexperienced.

- **Respond quickly.** One of the most meaningful ways that a chief executive can honor board members and acknowledge their vital role is by being responsive to their communications. Every chief executive is probably familiar with the feeling of placing 10 calls to a prospective donor, only to be told, "I didn't have anything to tell you now, so I didn't return your call." It is not good business for the chief executive to delay responding to the request or message of a board member simply because there is no news to report. Board members deserve to be in the know, even if it means that they are aware that no progress has been made on an issue since the last communication.

- **Be thoughtful.** Being responsive does not mean that requests from board members must be acted upon immediately. However, chief executives should acknowledge questions or requests when received and make a commitment about the action that will be taken to respond. The chief executive should set an example of responsiveness and work with the board chair to underscore the importance of board accountability to the organization.

- **Consider special challenges.** Chief executives need to consider time of day, common language, and cultural differences when communicating with board members located in other parts of the globe. Scheduling a teleconference at an hour that is convenient for a state-side meeting may be very early or very late for those on another continent. Being sensitive to the cultural observances of all board members is also important. Scheduling organizational events or meetings during religious holidays should be avoided.

WHEN IS IT THE "RIGHT" TIME?

Giving timely information is a sign that the chief executive has his or her finger on the pulse of the organization and its operating environment, respects those who need the information to consider issues and take action, and understands the importance of reflection and careful thought to produce the best results.

Board members need time before meetings to read and review reports, minutes, and other materials. The chief executive should be thoughtful about keeping information concise, organizing it in a logical fashion with a memo that previews the material, and allowing at least a week for review. The same rule of thumb applies to committee meetings. Minutes should be compiled and sent within a few weeks of the meeting, while the experience is fresh, with action items highlighted.

When it comes to board engagement, absence does not always make the heart grow fonder. It often makes the heart grow colder. If the chief executive's only communication with the board relates to board or committee meetings, some board members may file the organization in long-term memory. It is prudent to reach out to board members regularly to remind them that they are part of the family and that the organization counts on and values their presence of mind each day of the year, not just at board or committee meetings. Unless an issue is complex and needs to be shared between meetings, these touching-base communications should be short and to the point.

When it comes to bad news, the sooner the chief executive shares it the better. Some chief executives were caught off guard in the recent economic recession, watching their cash flow tighten and hoping that a reversal of their organization's fortune was right around the corner. These chief executives held the bad news from their board thinking that sharing it would be premature and impact the enthusiasm of the board or their impression of the chief executive's skill in financial management.

While keeping a positive organizational atmosphere is important, many of the chief executives that delayed or neglected sharing bad news about their organization's finances unnecessarily put their organization and its service recipients at risk. In some cases, certain programs were curtailed or discontinued. In other instances, the lack of timely communication on this critical issue resulted in the loss of the organization.

The chief executives who rang the alarm early on and tied the impact of the poor economy to negative impacts on the organization's mission likely saw their board address challenges with urgency and a clear commitment to pick up an oar and row the boat together through the choppy waters.

Times of crisis are the most important times of all for the board chair and chief executive to be on the same page. The more critical the challenge, the less likely the organization will be able to weather the storm if there is a lack of agreement among its top leadership.

> *In this era of e-mail, blogging, texting, and social networking, it is worth remembering that information may be transmitted electronically or on paper, but meaningful communication happens in person.*

COMMUNICATING SENSITIVE ISSUES

When information being shared is in response to a crisis or public policy initiative that requires quick action or analysis, the chief executive should consult with the board chair immediately to determine how to frame the information, who should receive it, and how to request action in a way that underscores the urgency of the situation and its potential impact. In consultation with the board, the chief executive should have anticipated situations that may require quick decision making and information sharing and have the policies and processes in place to address multiple situations. Of course, it is not possible to expect that every decision requiring quick action will have a policy in place to guide its outcome. In these cases, the chief executive can support the chair in decision making by framing the issue based upon the organization's mission, health, and well-being: "What action must we take to best serve the organization and our mission?"

For example, an organization's clients may depend on a state-funded program whose budget is cut in the late hours of a legislative session. If the board has approved position statements on a variety of public policy issues affecting the organization and designed a process for taking action between board meetings, then situations that require quick action — like this one — can be addressed with optimum impact.

Similarly, when an employee tells the chief executive that he or she has been subjected to off-color jokes from a co-worker, the organization is best equipped to handle the situation if it has comprehensive employee policies, developed in concert with and approved by the board.

Then there's the new board member who wants the organization to feature a political candidate at its fundraiser right before the election. Having a code of ethics will go a long way in heading off situations that can bring potential risk to the organization.

Even with the best plans, most organizations must answer tough questions from the public or the media at one time or another. A well-thought-out process developed and approved by the board can help to manage an organization's remaining opportunities to resolve the situation and recover, rehabilitate, or retain reputation. Even when there is no emergency, the chief executive's failure to provide timely information on pressing issues can end in difficulties for the board. Once the chief executive has given the board information or briefed it on an issue, he or she must keep up to date and share ongoing developments immediately, not at the next board meeting. When the board has one set of information and the chief executive has another, the situation can lead to confusion, frustration, and hard feelings.

In summary, in determining how to respond to sensitive issues, the chief executive should consider the following:

- **What is the key issue?** A complex situation generally has one or two critical issues, along with extraneous issues. While all may need to be considered, be sure to focus on the most pressing first.

- **Are there established policies or practices that could provide guidance?** Have them available to the decision makers for the discussion.

- **Is there a precedence that relates to the current issue at hand?** Even if not exactly the same, issues that relate to the problem being discussed need to be understood.

- **What's the timeframe for responding to this issue?** The decision makers need to understand if the problem is a crisis that needs an immediate response or one that could be researched, considered, and more carefully determined at a future time.

- **Who needs to be involved in making the response/decision?** For many situations, the board chair is needed. However, if the issue relates to an employee relations issue, sometimes the HR or personnel committee chair might be more helpful.

Times of crisis are the most important times of all for the board chair and chief executive to be on the same page. The more critical the challenge, the less likely the organization will be able to weather the storm if there is a lack of agreement among its top leadership.

Is your board prepared to address organizational concerns? Use this quick checklist as a starter:

Our organization has

☐ A public affairs or advocacy policy that details who, how and when the organization's public policy positions are developed and publicly presented

☐ An employee manual covering topics such as equal employment opportunity, harassment, conduct, employment separation, performance evaluation, and emergency response

☐ A code of ethics that covers conflict of interest, confidential and proprietary information, political contributions and activities, and relationships with donors

☐ A crisis communications policy. It is critical that the board and staff understand policies and processes in regard to the choice of appropriate representatives who speak on behalf of the organization in a time of crisis.

BoardSource has a treasure trove of downloadable sample policies on its Web site: www.boardsource.org.

FINDING AN EFFECTIVE FORMAT

Chief executives should put themselves in the board's shoes when choosing the most effective way to communicate. The best communicators are good empathizers. Most people don't like to receive e-mails or letters that go on and on without requesting a specific action, so the chances are that most board members don't either. These simple tips will help guide board communication format:

• Provide a table of contents, a cover memo, or hyperlinks when sending multiple pieces of information.

• Always state the purpose of the meeting or communication and why it is important. Close the loop by stating what is expected from the reader or participant.

• Be prepared for meetings, both formal and informal. Prepare an agenda, even for one-on-one meetings, so that time invested can be well spent. Anticipate questions or concerns, prepare board or committee chairs for possible challenges, and develop strategies ahead of time to deal with anticipated concerns.

• Use the telephone or face-to-face meetings when the information is sensitive or confidential. E-mails can easily be forwarded, sometimes unintentionally. Sensitive information can be shared with groups or individuals for whom it wasn't intended, posing a risk to the organization. Never share sensitive information on social networking sites.

- Schedule a personal meeting for important communications, such as an invitation to serve on the board or as a committee chair. Being asked via e-mail to join the board can send the message that the organization doesn't view board members as important participants in the organization or that potential board members don't deserve much investment of time. A personal approach makes the right impression.

- Be efficient when sending e-mail attachments. Avoid time-consuming graphics downloads, and compile individual documents into one. Or post large documents or meeting packages on an organization intranet and send an e-mail notification with a summary of the materials, what is expected of the board member, and the link and password.

- While regular communication is important, avoid incessant updates about trivial issues. Board members are busy people, too, and a constant flow of information that they are not certain how to use will only train them to ignore, delete, or delay reading all messages from the organization. All staff in the organization should follow this professional behavior.

- Do research carefully and have confidence in the sources. Providing incomplete or inaccurate information to board members is risky business.

WHAT THE TWEET IS THIS? — NEW FORMATS FOR COMMUNICATION

Facebook, Twitter, YouTube, Vimeo, LinkedIn, Flickr, Digg, MySpace, Google Buzz, Stumble Upon…the list of new and emerging social networking venues is nearly endless. The opportunities and pitfalls can be daunting to the chief executive who is working to keep abreast of the latest communication trends and methods.

It is astonishing, however, that hundreds of millions of individuals engage in information/opinion sharing via social media every day. Many of those individuals are board members and nonprofit organization staff interested in particular causes. It is critical that chief executives recognize the importance of this new communication format and learn as much as they can about using it effectively to benefit the organization.

Integrating use of social networking venues into the organization's existing communication formats provides board members with the opportunity to communicate in a way they feel most comfortable with (if they are social media users), or an opportunity for board members not familiar with this format to learn a new skill, if they wish. One organization held a social media orientation at a board meeting when their new cause page was unveiled, tying a new program to learning a new skill. Another organization conducted a briefing led by board members who use Facebook, LinkedIn, and Twitter to share news about issues and new information important to the organization. One board member explained that as she was preparing for a big fundraising event, she posted information every few days or so regarding fundraising progress, shared stories about individuals the organization helped, and made appeals for sponsorships, volunteers, and in-kind contributions as needs arose to support the event.

Reality, however, will dictate that most organizations have users and nonusers and the chief executive must remain vigilant in making certain to consider the best format for communicating with specific board members individually and the board as a whole.

There is no doubt that social networking puts communication power directly into the hands of the people in a way that nothing before ever has. Chief executives are well-advised to urge the board to develop and adopt social media guidelines for engagement or a social media policy covering areas from dealing with a compliment or complaint to an employee or board member who just posted something inappropriate or sensitive.

PROMOTING RESULTS-ORIENTED COMMUNICATION

Most successful companies train their salespeople on how to sell, not how to present. The same can be said for successful nonprofit organizations. Board members can be the organization's best salespeople, but often the difference between presenting and selling is not understood. It is not enough for board members simply to raise visibility for the organization in the community unless they produce measurable results in terms of donors, volunteers, and service recipients. Without results, little has been gained by preparing board members to speak knowledgeably about the organization.

Expecting board members to understand the organization's mission and be willing to promote the organization in the community is a reasonable starting point. The chief executive can build the impact of this expectation by creating results-oriented communications. How many donors, volunteers, or service recipients have board members secured for the organization? Are these success stories featured at board meetings? Is it clear that "closing the loop" with community contacts is expected among staff and board members? When the chief executive and board chair model results-oriented behavior and reinforce it in meetings and personal interactions with board members, it can go a long way toward building the board's comfort level in promoting the organization.

There is similar value to closing the loop when it comes to the chief executive's personal and professional interactions with the board. Productive meetings and one-on-one conversations should conclude with a list of action items, a timeframe for acting and reporting, and a reference to the purpose or importance of the action.

The chief executive is the primary architect in establishing results-oriented communication and managing the flow of information to board and staff members who are accountable for taking action. Follow-up information should be timely, specific, and acknowledge those responsible for taking next steps. The following tactics support results-oriented communication:

- Distribute meeting minutes in a timely fashion.

- Remind individual board members of their follow-up commitments and offer assistance well in advance of deadlines. Operating in a crisis mode — "This is due tomorrow!" — without having checked in at other points along the way is stressful to board members and affects the results.

- Provide support to board members in completing tasks.

- Provide new and emerging information related to assigned tasks as soon as it becomes available.

- Alert the board chair when board members who have volunteered for tasks have disappeared from the radar and might negatively affect the results of the team effort.

VIEW FROM THE BOARD CHAIR

Frequent and effective communications play a key role in developing engaged board members. They need to understand the organization's mission and key activities and then personalize this learning with their own experiences. The challenge is to provide the information in the right format.

For example, a statewide nonprofit began issuing monthly e-mail communications to all board members to build their general understanding about the organization. The message included past and upcoming activities, public service announcements, research findings, and more. The information was very thorough — too much for the average board member to digest easily and quickly. Many board members either deleted the e-mail or filed it away without reading it. At board meetings, it was evident that most members weren't benefiting from the information. The remedy was a one-page executive overview written as if it might be the only part the board member reads, with intriguing summary data to draw attention to the attachment. This approach satisfied those just wanting a general understanding of what was happening but also gave more details to those who wanted them.

Here are some practical tips that can help facilitate communication between board and chief executive and among board members:

- Wallet cards with phone numbers of key contacts help you connect with each other easily.

- Reminders to board members about upcoming events.

- If board members miss meetings, a "sorry we missed you" note with the information shared at the meeting helps keep them connected.

- Pictures help tell the story. Take photos of the services you offer, clients you help, volunteers in action, and share them with board members. Seeing is believing!

- Web sites with a designated section just for board members can be used to post critical information, calendars of activities, even meeting materials. But you may need to send board members an e-mail directing them that new information has been posted. Don't assume board members are regularly checking such sites.

- Take into account the differences in technology aptitude. Some members will be knowledgeable about the various social media venues — and others won't have a clue. Offer brief training sessions for the uninitiated to learn about these newer approaches.

VIEW FROM THE CHIEF EXECUTIVE'S DESK

Many times in my experience as a chief executive, I've needed to broach a sensitive topic with a board member. One of the most common relates to securing a personal contribution from a board member who hasn't acted on this responsibility or request. My organization requires that board members give at a meaningful level within their own means, but once I had a board member drive up in her Mercedes, wearing a fur coat, and tell me, "Sorry I haven't given my annual gift yet. It's been a tough year."

In situations like this one — when a board member failed to make a personal contribution — the problem usually can be traced to communication. The board member might not understand the depth of the expectations placed on him or her, and that failing to fulfill these expectations takes away a vote of confidence within the organization. Sensitive topics like this one are easier to approach if the chief executive is intentional and up front in communication with the board member.

In these instances I've found success in keeping the response to the prospective donor on a positive note, indicating that it is a board policy and a specific responsibility for board members to give. There are rare times that we don't reach the 100 percent goal. I explain that nongiving board members are contacted by our nominating committee, a personal call to inquire about the obstacles they may be encountering in completing one or more basic requirements of board service. Often this interaction results in a recommitment to the organization. Other times, board members have chosen to be reassigned to a committee or other responsibility until they are able to fully participate as a board member and role model to our constituents and supporters.

My board chair and I strategize how best to introduce a conversation about the importance of annual board giving, or any other sensitive topic, depending on the relationship we both have with an individual board member. We make a point of being specific about the board's expectations and policies. As testimony to the value of intentional communication, I've never had one of these conversations end poorly when I use this approach.

PARTNERSHIP TIPS TO REMEMBER

- Always consider when, where, how, and how much to communicate.

- Complement information generated within the organization with information on the external environment.

- Balance the time you invest in gaining knowledge with the time needed to make it useful to yourself and the board.

- Remember that either over abundance or a scarcity of information can create pitfalls for you and the board.

- Solicit the board chair's advice in determining what information needs to go to all board members, some board members, or no one.

- Remember that the most meaningful communication happens in person, not through paper or electronic media.

- Touch base with board members every week or so with news about recent accomplishments or a new discovery in the field, a newsletter, or a specific request for securing a volunteer or in-kind product or service.

- Share what keeps you up at night so board members are aware of how you've sized up the organization's challenges and opportunities and can be better partners in tackling the issues together.

- Have policies and plans in place that indicate the rules of engagement for board and staff across multiple social networks and the representatives that are appropriate to communicate on behalf of your organization in public forums, including social media venues.

- Expect board members to understand the organization's mission and be willing to promote the organization in the community. Prepare board members to do the job successfully through offering a thorough orientation program that covers the results-oriented goals the organization is working toward and by helping each board member find his or her own personal story or connection to the mission.

- Model results-oriented behaviors by concluding meetings and one-on-one interactions with a list of action items, a timeframe for acting and reporting, and a reference to the purpose or importance of the action.

CHAPTER 5

FACILITATE A BALANCE IN ROLES AND RESPONSIBILITIES

Communicate board members' roles and expectations — and understand your own.

Chief executives who inspire their boards to move from adequate to extraordinary recognize that the board–executive partnership is a complex balance of responsibilities and expectations, not a command-and-control relationship. Questions about who does what sometimes have no clear-cut answers. One thing is certain: No matter how visionary and competent the chief executive may be, simply handing out scripts and marching orders will not motivate the board to perform at its full potential. A chief executive who is too heavy handed deprives the organization of the creativity and energy of a fully engaged board. A board that is dominated by a chief executive lacks the autonomy and authority to carry out many of its governance responsibilities.

CLARIFYING THE BOARD'S ROLE

Micromanagement, misdirection, and disengagement of board members often result from a misunderstanding of roles. For this reason, it is in the chief executive's best interest to facilitate the board's knowledge and understanding of its responsibilities and expectations and to fulfill his or her own responsibilities with strength and confidence. For board members, this learning process is the best preparation for success, and the chief executive should be an active participant.

One organization includes a discussion of board and staff roles in its orientation program along with informational material on the topic in its volunteer handbook. It encourages both board and staff to keep the focus of volunteer leaders on areas of policy, resource development, and strategy. This well-put focus enhances the board–staff partnership versus duplicating staff's responsibilities for implementation and execution.

ADOPTING OR DISTINGUISHING RESPONSIBILITIES

As a starting point, every chief executive must be well informed about the framework in which nonprofit governing boards are required to operate. Governance involves basic responsibilities, and accomplishing them requires the chief executive to provide structure and information and promote an environment of inquiry.

Chief executives can begin this process of facilitation and education by giving new board members information about nonprofit governance developed by BoardSource, the state attorney general's office, or a local or state nonprofit association or resource center. An outside speaker on governance at the annual board orientation or a board meeting can help drive home the point that the board has a responsibility to the community as well as to the nonprofit itself.

No matter how visionary and competent the chief executive may be, simply handing out scripts and marching orders will not motivate the board to perform at its full potential.

One organization begins board meetings with a reminder of the basic responsibilities of board members. After the board chair calls the meeting to order, he reviews the duties that are specific to how board members must operate while conducting business on behalf of the organization:

Duty of Care: *As board members you must be actively engaged in the organization's activities and understand its mission.*

Duty of Loyalty: *As board members you should act solely in the best interest of the organization and follow conflict-of-interest policies to avoid any tangible or perceived actions that could result in personal gain.*

Duty of Obedience: *As board members you must be committed to the mission of the organization and be familiar with and follow your articles, bylaws, and policies as well as state or federal laws applicable to the organization and your position.*

Sometimes the chief executive has to be involved in board member responsibilities to make things happen and manage the process. A quick review of the board's basic responsibilities (see Appendix 5 for a list of them) will show that in most areas it is appropriate, if not vital, for the chief executive to play a pivotal role in supporting the board in doing its job. For example, for the board to enhance the organization's public standing, the chief executive must report on organizational accomplishments by connecting them to mission and then give board members specific messages they can share with the community. The annual audit and periodic internal financial statements are essential tools for the board in carrying out its fiduciary responsibilities, yet neither one can be produced without the chief executive's assistance or acted on without his or her guidance.

Perhaps the only major board responsibilities in which the chief executive does not participate are selecting, evaluating, and determining the compensation of the chief executive. Even then, the executive should be involved in succession planning, including reminding the board of its role and recruiting and developing staff that have leadership potential. See Chapter 7 for more information about the chief executive's role in supporting the board in developing leadership succession plans.

DEFINING STANDARDS

In addition to their governance responsibilities, board members are expected to follow certain principles that are essential to effective participation. The organization may have orientation and meeting attendance requirements, or it may specify a range of hours per month that board members are expected to dedicate to board service. Many organizations spell out fundraising expectations, including the requirement that board members make annual contributions according to their own means (see Appendix 1 for an example of board member expectations).

Board members should understand and agree to these standards of behavior before they commit to board service. A good time to introduce them is during the initial board recruitment call. Reviewing each expectation and getting a verbal or signed commitment helps ensure that a candidate knows what it takes to be a successful board member.

For the board to embrace and own its standards for behavior, the chief executive is well advised to facilitate a review and discussion of current board practices at least annually. This discussion may be handled most effectively in a smaller group, such as the governance committee or executive committee, because these settings offer enough time for thoughtful consideration. The results and any proposed revisions to expectations for board members can be presented at a full board meeting to gain additional feedback. This process has two secondary benefits: It reminds board members — old and new — what the organization expects from them, and it gives board members an opportunity to ask for clarification. Standard practices may be updated with discussion and adjustment to changing needs.

Board Self-Assessment is a tool available from BoardSource that helps the board reflect on how well it is meeting its governance responsibilities and provides structure for establishing a common understanding of its roles and responsibilities, as well as for discovering critical areas for improvement. Visit www.boardsource.org for detailed information about this resource.

HELPING THE BOARD ASSESS ITS PERFORMANCE

Strong governance has become increasingly more important in recent years with a series of high-profile nonprofit scandals, ongoing Senate Finance Committee hearings about nonprofit issues, and the revisions to the IRS 990 form.

Just as the chief executive can help the board measure his or her performance through a formalized review process, so can he or she help facilitate a similar process by which the board evaluates its overall performance and the performance of individual board members. This is a way for chief executives to make sure that the board is an asset, rather than a liability. Paying attention to governance structure, composition, oversight, strategies, and policies helps to strengthen governance.

One organization used the *Nonprofit Governance Index 2010* to develop a board performance report card (see Appendix 6 for a sample report card) for its organization. Each board member graded the board's performance in several areas including fundraising, strategic planning, financial oversight, and mission knowledge. Grades were averaged and compared to those of 780 other board members completing the survey nationwide. Also included was the average of grades given their board's performance by chief executives from 978 different nonprofit organizations.

This exercise provides a good basis for benchmarking board performance, along with a side-by-side comparison to the grades chief executives give their boards and how boards rate themselves. Discussion and planning about ways to raise the board's "grade point average" follow examination of their report card.

Another nonprofit organization chose to encourage stronger involvement from its board members by clearly identifying *levels of performance* for each of the stated board responsibilities. A matrix was developed to indicate the various board functions with behavioral descriptions of three levels of participation: Threshold, Full, and Exceptional.

For example,

STEWARDSHIP OF TALENT AND TREASURE

Threshold Participation:
- Personally make annual contribution
- Leverage gifts/in-kind contributions

Full Participation:
- Meet Threshold Participation level expectations
- Contribute to and attend at least one fundraising event
- Identify and solicit financial contributions and participation in fundraising from others

Exceptional Participation:
- Meet Full Participation level expectations
- Contribute to and attend more than one fundraising event
- Help identify new sources of revenue
- Provide professional expertise for operations

By setting out these levels, board members were able to evaluate their own performance and understand how to strengthen their support for the organization.

See Appendix 7, "Sample Board of Directors' Performance Matrix," for more details.

SETTING EXPECTATIONS FOR THE CHIEF EXECUTIVE

The board's expectations of the chief executive generally are expressed in a job description — not the same description the search committee used in recruitment, but a new, working document that reflects the goals of the strategic plan and the ever-changing challenges and opportunities faced by nonprofit organizations and their leaders.

Having an obvious path of action and regular progress checks is not something that a chief executive should wait patiently for the board to provide. A clear set of expectations and measurements by which to chart progress helps him or her consciously invest time in fulfilling the will of the board and bringing greatest benefit to the organization. The chief executive should take the lead in drafting the goals and measurable objectives for his or her job duties within the authority that the board has granted.

The chief executive can use the expectations outlined in the job description to facilitate working with the board, including

- **Managing time and priorities.** Consult it as a guide to sorting through multiple priorities and managing time.

- **Keeping the job description relevant.** Add notes about new developments or longer-term goals that may be bookmarks for discussion during the annual performance review or as a springboard for a board or committee discussion.

- **Structuring business discussions with the board chair.** Use it as an agenda format for regular meetings with the board chair. In addition to sharing updates on current organizational issues, the two leaders may want to tackle the job description and annual goals one section at a time over a series of regular one-on-one meetings.

- **Sharing progress reports with the board.** Share areas of focus with the full board through regular review of the strategic plan, a presentation to the board about major issues and challenges, and regular executive reports at board meetings. This technique reinforces the chief executive's major concerns and serves as a constant reminder of the types of activities that the executive handles on a regular basis.

Helping the Board Assess the Chief Executive's Performance

At a recent conference of small to midsized nonprofit organizations, an informal poll of chief executives showed that nearly half had not participated in a formal review of their performance in the past year. There has been improvement in these numbers with the introduction of the new IRS 990 reporting requirements, which put focus on the process by which a chief executive is evaluated and compensated by the board. BoardSource's *Nonprofit Governance Index 2010* reports that 71 percent of nonprofits surveyed conduct a formal, written performance evaluation of their chief executive.

While a chief executive might assume, "I must be doing OK if no one has said anything otherwise," this is a dangerous assumption. Without a performance review, the executive is allowing the board, the staff, and the community to judge his or her performance without a set of clearly defined expectations to guide the assessment.

Although some boards take the initiative in scheduling a performance review, the chief executive should not wait for the board to make the first move. He or she should structure a formal review once annually. At a minimum, this process should involve the board chair. Other participants might include the immediate past chair, the incoming chair, and some committee chairs and board officers. Many performance reviews are handled by governance or executive committees, which usually are composed of board officers and committee chairs.

One of the most powerful tools to help the chief executive is an effective and frank performance discussion.

A healthy performance review is about much more than compensation. Among other things, it supports the chief executive's capacity for working with the board by gathering information about the accomplishment of measurable objectives, assessing organizational issues and challenges for the year ahead, and setting objectives for the annual work plan. To give the review session coaching value, the chief executive should prepare a self-assessment in advance and set aside at least two hours for this important discussion. It is important to ensure confidentiality by explaining that the purpose is to collect information that will be analyzed as group data. The performance review team will find this wider perspective useful in shaping meaningful feedback that helps the chief executive improve his or her success in working with the board.

In between performance reviews, board members should provide ongoing feedback to the chief executive. For example, one board member noticed the chief executive commenting on the value of feedback from committee members during a brainstorming session. The board member pointed out that the spirit of enthusiasm was dampened and board members felt less apt to provide their thoughts when the chief executive was evaluating their value with comments like "good idea," "that won't work," "we tried that before," etc. It takes courage to give a chief executive, especially a seasoned one, constructive comments on his or her performance. The chief executive should have the presence of mind to listen carefully to what might be subtle but meaningful coaching, thank the board member for caring enough to offer feedback, and find ways to implement the good advice in behavior or work action.

Assessment of the Chief Executive is a tool available from BoardSource that clarifies the chief executive's responsibilities, job expectations, and annual goals; captures the board's perception of the executive's strengths, limitations, and overall performance; and fosters growth and development of the chief executive and the organization.

Visit www.boardsource.org for detailed information about this resource and a host of others dedicated to the evaluation of the chief executive.

Noticing the Warning Signs

Effective partnerships involve give and take, trusting communication, and enjoyment of working together on common goals. The chief executive will know when the balance is healthy and productive because the partnership will focus on the organization's mission, with both the chief executive and the board engaged in bringing their appropriate skills and expertise to bear on the desired results.

If the partnership shows any of the following symptoms of imbalance, it's time to take a step back (and revisit other chapters of this book) to understand where the proper adjustments need to be made in order to get things back on track:

- The chief executive gives orders to the board rather than discussing issues and programs together to determine the best course of action. The message: The chief executive is the boss, and board members are subordinates.

- The chief executive interacts with the board only at board or committee meetings. The message: The board is only needed to rubber-stamp decisions, and its value is nonexistent aside from showing up to be counted.

- The chief executive performs his or her duties without the benefit of feedback from the board, though board members talk among themselves about the executive's performance. The message: No feedback is good feedback — or is it? The chief executive is in a vulnerable position, with no clearly defined expectations as guidance.

- The chief executive — and maybe even the board chair — makes unilateral decisions. The message: There's no careful thought about how developments that affect the organization should be shared with board members so they are kept in the loop and ready to make informed decisions when called upon.

- The chief executive conceals information. The message: The executive is in a tough spot, craves power, or needs a tool to deflect communication about uncomfortable issues.

- Board members are demoralized because some of their colleagues are so disengaged that they rarely show up for meetings, respond to messages, or bring any measurable value to the cause. The message: The chief executive hasn't nudged board leadership about the negative impact that underperforming board members have on the organization.

On the flip side, weak or passive leadership on the chief executive's part will also spur a variety of problems. When the executive is disorganized, unprepared, or avoids dealing with difficult situations, he or she invites the board chair (or even committee chairs) to be domineering, left to steer the organization alone through choppy waters without the benefit of a fully functioning compass or map.

VIEW FROM THE BOARD CHAIR

The balance between the role of the board and that of the chief executive continues to be a challenge. Most board members understand they are to help the organization determine strategic issues such as "Are we doing the right things to achieve our mission?" We all must frequently remind ourselves to avoid delving into details that are not the primary focus of a board. Board members are not management and tactical activities are generally determined by staff members.

However, boards have been torn between fulfilling their duties to provide appropriate financial oversight with their other more strategic governance responsibilities. In *Govern More, Manage Less* (BoardSource, 2010), Cathy A. Trower notes that "Nonprofit and private sector experts suggest that effective governance requires an appropriate balance around compliance and performance; and fiduciary oversight, strategic foresight, and generative insight."

To assist the board in achieving this balance, the chief executive should use the strategic plan at board and committee meetings to frame discussions. When seeking board input, ask questions with a strategic viewpoint in mind. For example, if the chief executive is discussing the need for new software for tracking donors, which of these questions would keep the board focused strategically?

- "We have researched xx system. It can do these things and costs this much. Do you agree that the organization should purchase this new software to address our donor tracking needs?"

- "Here are some of the needs that staff members have identified for a new donor tracking system. We would like to have board input to ensure that we've considered other potential requirements and future uses of such data to address organizational goals. What thoughts do you have that we should consider in this purchase?"

Obviously the board may need details at some point in terms of authorizing a major purchase, but many board members don't have the technical background to choose a system or evaluate if the cost is appropriate. Asking for input that encourages open thinking will generally allow for more strategic discussions.

Moving to a more focused and specific activity that requires board involvement is that of the performance review of the chief executive.

One of the most powerful tools to help the chief executive is an effective and frank performance discussion. Organizations handle performance differently, and there is no perfect system that will ensure effective communication on this potentially sensitive subject. The chief executive can smooth the way by welcoming feedback from board leaders on how they perceive he or she is addressing the responsibilities of the job. Being direct about performance issues is a challenge for many people. It is human nature to be more comfortable giving good news than dealing with concerns. And in a nonprofit environment where board members have limited exposure to the chief executive, they may be hesitant to share their perspective, knowing that they don't have a full understanding of the executive's daily performance. If the chief executive comes across as defensive — demanding multiple examples to substantiate board members' comments, for example — board input will be stifled.

A few years ago, I was working with a chief executive who was fairly argumentative when presented with comments about her performance that were in any way less than glowing. Based on my role with the organization, it was my task to conduct her performance evaluation. I told her that I believed my thoughts about her performance could help her improve her outcomes, but that I didn't have strong backup to support my point of view. I asked her if she wanted this information and would be willing to consider it potentially valid even if I couldn't come up with multiple examples. She appeared shocked at my question but then said that she did wish to hear my thoughts. Because I invited her to ask for my guidance, she was more open to listening, and the discussion proceeded with good results. But the chief executive would not have benefited from what I had to say if she had made it too difficult for me to say it — and the big losers would have been she and the organization.

Most board members are uncomfortable in dealing with conflict. It's up to the chief executive to make it OK for board members to provide performance feedback without feeling like they're on a witness stand. Ask clarifying questions to better understand the input, but try not to be defensive: "I hear that you think I was too rash in my reactions to X situation. Could you help me understand how you believe I might have responded differently to have a better outcome?" This approach conveys openness to learning and keeps the focus positive.

VIEW FROM THE CHIEF EXECUTIVE'S DESK

As a chief executive, I always strived to put serious effort into my responsibility to frame the organization's mission, direction, and priorities into all my formal and informal communications with the board. I knew that the work of our organization was pretty serious stuff. Creating social change in a complicated and sometimes uncooperative world is a big and important order to fill.

Why, then, did I hear comments from board members like "I don't feel a connection to the work we're doing," "Can't we talk about anything other than fundraising?" or "This really isn't as much fun as I thought it would be"?

I aired my confusion and frustration among trusted colleagues and board members and learned that projects, programs, goals, budgets, and fundraising targets can weigh heavily on a board member's shoulders. Add to this the actual governance duties of care, loyalty, due diligence, and fiduciary responsibility, and the life force can be sapped right out of them. The fun seems to be taken out of making a difference.

In my serious quest to prepare the board to be successful, I neglected the very human element of fun. There's a kid in all of us that needs to play, and board members are no different. Chief executives need to have fun, too, and find ways to lighten our load in the midst of our serious responsibilities.

In looking to introduce a little fun into the serious responsibilities of the board, our organization developed some avenues that reinforce play, creativity, socialization, and experiential learning. Here are some examples:

1. Include an expectation in the board members' job description that encourages fun, such as, "Have fun, learn, teach, and share in successes and failures. Provide honest, constructive feedback to benefit the success of the organization."

2. Ask board members to complete a biography, including the question, "What is one thing that people wouldn't know about you that you'd like to share?" On several occasions, we've sent bios in advance of the board meeting, along with a treasure hunt quiz that encouraged everyone to read them. We offered silly prizes for the board members getting the highest scores on their treasure hunt.

3. Review financial statements using a word search puzzle approach. Our treasurer asks board members to "circle the number at the bottom of page two in the center column" and "three columns over to the left of the special events line," and so forth. Once the board's financials are all "circled up," the treasurer explains how and why the circled numbers are important.

4. Invite a board member or two along to an awards program, Association of Fundraising Professionals Philanthropy Day, or a reception held by a local community foundation or corporate supporter. Such an event is a nice social and networking opportunity for the board member in a relaxed atmosphere, and the organization has expanded the number of PR agents it has to work the crowd to promote the organization.

5. Organize an optional Dutch-treat dinner after a board meeting. Choose an affordable but nice location close to the board meeting site. Board members who need to interact, ask questions, or get to know others better will appreciate this opportunity.

6. Ask board members to give welcoming or closing remarks at service programs, including volunteer training, donor appreciation luncheons, grant award presentations, or special events. Just about any time people gather in the name of our organization and its services, there is an opportunity to involve a board member. Not only do they enjoy representing the organization, they also can participate in the service program, learn more about us, and meet the clients we serve.

7. Give board members a handful of calls to make to recent donors, to just say thanks.

8. Organize informal get-togethers at a nearby coffee shop where all board members are invited but participation is optional. These gatherings — scheduled periodically in the morning, midafternoon, or late afternoon — offer an escape from the office for conversation about what the organization is doing well, what it can improve, or other big-picture topics.

Board members are people, too. When they enjoy the time they give to the organization, they're more likely to stay and give their best.

PARTNERSHIP TIPS TO REMEMBER

- Provide an annual orientation workshop or presentation for all board members (not just new board members) covering expectations, roles, and responsibilities in governing the organization.

- Set standards for board performance including expectations for meeting attendance, financial, and time contributions.

- Take the lead in drafting the short-term and long-term measurable goals that you are responsible to the organization to achieve. Use the strategic plan as your framework. This document can serve as basis for your performance review.

- Facilitate an annual formal review of your performance and include the board chair in the meeting.

- Keep the board on track by using the strategic plan as a framework for board and committee meetings and actions.

- Remember to introduce a little fun into the serious work of the board by developing activities that reinforce play, creativity, and socialization.

CHAPTER 6
STRUCTURE THE BOARD'S WORK

Mobilize board members with purposeful organization and process.

Bringing together a group of people with diverse talents, interests, and skills to work toward a common goal is no easy task. Structuring board members' work so that they are fully engaged in their governance role has been compared to herding cats. For the harried chief executive, this analogy may seem apt, albeit unfortunate, since there are no best practices or success stories to be adopted from the field of feline wrangling.

The structure and function of a nonprofit board differ from almost any other type of team or group. On most sports teams, for example, some members play unique roles, but all players share an interest in and knowledge of the sport and have skills that support success. Boards are built differently. Backgrounds and skill sets are diverse, and motivations and interests vary. And while board members determine policy through a deliberative process, they are encouraged to employ independent thinking in their board work. Boards rarely hold annual tryouts for positions, but instead, the best boards often have term limits; most of them fall in the range of two or three multiyear terms.

It may seem impossible to lead this well-intentioned group of individualists so that they focus on meaningful strategic thinking and deliberative collective action. A good starting point for structuring the board's work is an annual leadership survey that assesses board members' interest in continuing on the board, preferred committee assignments, and other current or desired commitments to the organization (see Appendix 8 for a sample survey). Equipped with this information about the board's potential, the chief executive, in partnership with the board chair, structures the board's work through his or her involvement in five areas: strategic planning, board nominations, board meetings, board committees, and donor development.

FINDING THE RIGHT BOARD MEMBERS

The chief executive is the primary keeper of the puzzle pieces that make up the character and skill set of the board, such as the status of board member contributions and board member participation in organization events and committee work. He or she should also have a good grasp of the action steps the board needs to take in the short term and the long term to carry out the organization's work plan and achieve its strategic objectives. For example, the chief executive may know that the giving officer of an important funder is planning to retire, which may interrupt the funding relationship with her organization and impact a critical program important to the organization. In this case, the chief executive may be looking to recruit someone within the funder's organization to join her organization's board or a committee.

If the organization is trying to increase foundation funding for their initiatives, identifying a potential board member with such knowledge would be very beneficial. Another example involves understanding the composition of the current board and the desire to secure representatives from new sources; a statewide entity might need a candidate from a territory that is not covered by existing membership. Determining skills and backgrounds necessary to enhance the support that board members can provide help focus the search for new board members.

> *The optimum results will come when the chief executive partners with the board in the nominating process to populate the board with members who are a good match with the organization's true needs.*

For these reasons, the chief executive must play a meaningful, involved role in the board nomination process: determining what types of members the board needs, recruiting prospects, participating in the interview process, and inviting them to serve as candidates for election or re-election.

Some nonprofits embrace the tenet that to ensure a balance of power, it is best not to have the board chair involved in nominations. This policy is a safeguard against a board chair having too much authority in the process. It also allows the governance committee to discuss officer nominations without having the board chair in the room. Of course, the board chair can suggest potential candidates for the board.

Many chief executives leave board nominations to a select group of officers or a governance committee, viewing the process as the work of a secret society of the board and resigning themselves to living with whatever candidates the board advances. Then there are chief executives who take full control of board nominations, often wandering haphazardly through their communities adding people they favor without regard to the organization's strategic needs or the board's ownership of the nominating process. Neither approach is a good one. The optimum results will come when the chief executive partners with the board in the nominating process to populate the board with members who are a good match with the organization's true needs. The chief executive is responsible for

- staffing the committee; this is not a job for another staff member

- developing the meeting schedule and agendas with the committee chair, taking into account the organization's needs, current board profile, diversity goals, term limits, optimum board size, and inactive board members who need to be removed

- helping the committee chair keep the committee on track, avoiding a race for each member to recruit the most friends whether or not they suit the board's needs

- keeping diligence about timely follow-up on assigned tasks; the chief executive should remind the committee chair to continue the momentum between meetings and issue reminders about pending tasks

A board profile is a useful first step in the nominating process. The profile data give the chief executive the opportunity to match the organization's needs against the interests, talents, level of commitment, and resources a board candidate can bring to the table.

PREPARING THE BOARD TO OPEN DOORS

Board members have many contributions to offer, and it is up to the chief executive and board chair — working as a team with a common message — to help them understand how they can bring value to the organization. Opening doors to needed resources is one of the greatest opportunities a board member can provide. Beyond personal financial support, fundraising is a key component of board responsibilities. Some people are comfortable making the contacts with potential donor sources directly, while others are less willing or able to do so. Together, the chief executive and board chair (and development committee chair, if one exists) must clarify each board member's ability to assist with this critical function and provide training to those who are willing but lack the skill or knowledge.

See Appendix 9 for a sample board member profile, which asks board members to rate their ability to provide financial support, people to help, and other contacts for resources to help the organization. This self-reported information from board members is a good starting point for the chief executive and board chair to have specific conversations with every board member about how they can help bring resources to the organization and what support they need to be successful.

Access to resources can be much broader than just the financial links. Letting board members know the needs of the organization can get their creative juices going. In some cases, links to grant-writing skills, advocacy influence with public policymakers, and in-kind donations of products and services are all valuable assets that board members may be able to provide if they understand what's needed and expected. Working in partnership with the committee chair, the chief executive should ask board members to put thought into developing a list of individuals, organizations, or companies that might share a common interest in the mission, the desire to provide community service, or the benefit of gaining leadership experience in community affairs.

The chief executive should make it clear that board members are matchmakers on behalf of the organization. Donor development, as with any relationship, is rarely all sewn up in one interaction. Connecting people or groups that may meet each other's needs is a relatively simple task. The board member's job involves connecting with his or her contacts to find out if they are interested in learning more about the organization and arranging for an introductory, get-acquainted meeting with the board member and an organization representative who is experienced in calling on donors or supporters.

It is the job of the chief executive and the board to invite members of the community to support the organization. The simple act of doing this should be considered a success, and the notion that the introductory meeting is a failure if it doesn't result in an immediate contribution is counterproductive. Once prospective supporters have received the invitation, it is really up to them to determine their level of interest in pursuing the relationship further. The chief executive should orchestrate the follow-up, which should be outlined with the prospect at the close of the meeting to ensure that all parties agree where the new relationship is headed.

> *Donor development, as with any relationship, is rarely all sewn up in one interaction.*

GUIDING STRATEGIC PLANNING AND FOLLOW-THROUGH

When the chief executive sets the scene for effective planning, she helps provide the right framework for the board to structure its actions and fulfill its organizational responsibilities. A chief executive who is not "setting the table" in concert with the board chair to facilitate the completion of this responsibility is putting the board and the organization at some degree of risk.

A freestyle approach to the organization's focus will only result in confusion, frustration, and blurred roles between the board and chief executive. Most board members are good, caring human beings who need to find relevance and prove their value to the organization. The less that need is met, the more board members will try to find a direction that meets it, no matter how far off track it is from what needs to be done.

A strategic plan determines where an organization is going over the next several years, how it's going to get there, and how it will know if it got there or not. Working together, the chair and chief executive should outline the planning process, develop a timeline, and budget the resources needed. The strategic plan will help them chart what needs to be done and provide a solid basis from which board, committee, and staff goals and objectives flow.

The chief executive should work with the board chair to maintain the direction and inspiration of the strategic plan in the organization's everyday work. The chief executive (in collaboration with the board chair) has a few options for bringing focus to what needs to be done:

- Assign pieces of the strategic plan to specific committees. Build in strategic plan progress reports or discussion at each committee meeting and an overall progress report or discussion at board meetings. Highlight a "hit" and a "miss" from the strategic plan to discuss at each board meeting to get input.

- Ask board members to "adopt" a strategic priority and pledge their participation to goals and objectives and their attention in keeping themselves up to date on progress in the area they've adopted.

- Include strategic plan objectives in board committee work plans and staff job descriptions.

- Create a one-page "score card" of your organization's most important goals, challenges, and actions for the coming year. Include the score card with the materials provided to board members for study before each board and committee meeting. Provide a bullet point summary of progress for each issue that appears on the score card (see Appendix 10 for a sample score card). The score card also helps the board stay focused on the key issues that tie into the strategic plan.

MAXIMIZING BOARD POTENTIAL IN CHALLENGING TIMES

The loss of a key funder, a sharp downturn in the economy, a threat to the organization's reputation, or new competitor moving into an organization's service area are just some situations that introduce new challenges for the board to address.

While rarely pleasant to share, the chief executive who rings the alarm early and has prepared succinct and thorough background information regarding the issue is more likely to have a board that is willing to help than one who is overwhelmed and disappointed. The chief executive should structure communication in a way that is factual, but also positive in terms of the organization's ability to intervene early on and take opportunities to strengthen the organization in the process of tackling the challenge.

One organization suffered a dramatic decline in the usual level of support it received for its golf tournament. The economy was poor and many of its corporate sponsors were challenged as well. The sponsors started viewing golf events more as a luxury than a fundraising venue to support a charitable mission. The decline in support impacted the organization's ability to meet the growing demands of its clients. The chief executive prepared a historical review of the fundraising trends of her organization's event, a summary of trends being experienced by other golf events in the area, and the specific impact that the loss of revenue had on programs. The board chair asked board members to look at the situation with a "different set of eyes" because the world around us is changing so dramatically and quickly.

Because the board was invited to participate in addressing the challenge early on, was well prepared by the information provided by the chief executive, and was invited by the board chair to help "crack the nut," it responded with enthusiasm rather than fatigue and creativity rather than a lack of inspiration. Staff left the meeting with suggestions for budget cuts, ideas to build new features to the existing event, and even one introduction to a new funding source that had interest in the programs being impacted by the shortage in resources.

VIEW FROM THE BOARD CHAIR

With all the usual policy issues that must be recorded in board meeting minutes — including financial reports, committee reports, and updates from the chief executive and board chair — it can be a challenge to structure board meetings as strategic discussions rather than rubber-stamp events focused mainly on past history. If meetings are simply show-and-tell sessions, some board members may not show up unless they are presenting reports. This approach is the same as giving every student a bit part in the class play. They may all be present and feel included, but they seldom produce good drama.

The chief executive can help the board chair shift the culture of meetings from rubber-stamping to dynamic discussion. This culture shift may take some courage, since the outcome of the new and improved meetings will depend far less on a controlled, predictable agenda and far more on harnessing the unpredictable wisdom and passion of the board.

A good first step is for the chief executive to work with the board chair to move the committee reporting function to a consent agenda supported by written materials sent well in advance of the meeting. The consent agenda includes all items that require formal board approval but are not controversial, such as approval of the minutes from the last meeting, committee reports, and receipt of the past month's financial report and therefore require no discussion before a vote. It usually appears near the beginning of the meeting agenda to allow for any item to be moved to the meeting agenda for a full discussion if necessary. A consent agenda is a good motivator because it places more responsibility on board members to do their homework and actually read the materials provided to them prior to the meeting. Those board members who fulfill this important responsibility are not subjected to repetitive, routine recitations of information they have already covered!

Next, the chief executive and the board chair should encourage board members and committee chairs to submit high-impact issues for discussion. These issues may relate to long-term goals in the strategic plan or to a particular challenge that the organization or a committee is facing. For instance, the unexpected loss of a donor who has contributed 20 percent of the organization's revenue might trigger a rich discussion on the feasibility of replacing the revenue and what expenses to cut if resources aren't available to cover the loss. Another discussion might focus on strategies for adding diversity to the board. Catalytic questions — those that invite creativity and exploration and do not depend on data and logic to answer — help chief executives and board chairs instigate robust board discussions (see Appendix 2 for examples of catalytic questions).

A sample agenda for a high-impact board meeting follows:

HIGH-IMPACT BOARD OF DIRECTORS' AGENDA

(50+ percent of time allotted for strategic and policy discussion/action)

Agenda Topic	Leader	Format	Desired Results
Consent Agenda — minutes, committee reports, financial statements	Board chair	Full board	Board approval
Loss of Important Donation	Development chair	Full board problem solving	Strategy for specific actions to replace revenue/cut expenses
Becoming an Inclusive Board	Governance chair	Small groups brainstorm and report to full board	Clear vision for diversity, next steps, and long term-action plan
Financial Investment Policy — proposed	Treasurer	Presentation, discussion	Approval
Evaluation	Board chair	Feedback Form to gather feedback about the meeting's effectiveness in serving the organization's mission and optimal engagement of the board	Feedback for further improvement of board meeting effectiveness

See Appendix 11 for a sample Board of Directors Meeting Feedback Form.

MAKING DECISIONS IN THE BOARDROOM

When preparing the board to make optimal decisions during the deliberative process, the chief executive should remember these guiding principles:

- Research, prepare, and distribute in advance of meetings background information that puts all board members on a level playing field to participate in deliberative decision making.

- Touch base with key board members to learn their questions, concerns, and stances on important issues. One organization assigns key staff to connect with each committee chair one month in advance of the meeting to determine if there are issues to bring to the full board for discussion, problem solving, or opportunity exploration.

- Share background information about each of the issues for discussion with the board chair so that he or she is prepared and can address lingering concerns before a deliberative decision.

- Communicate your recommendations and the stance of related organizations or partner organizations on critical issues with board members informally and formally.

- Ask to participate in the discussion or present an executive analysis, which can point out how a particular issue or decision does or does not fit the organization's mission, strategic plan, and annual goals.

- Take time to discuss important board decisions with the board chair well in advance to learn his or her stance, share ideas, and fill in information gaps.

Even with the best advance work, board discussion of a critical issue may be sidetracked by intense emotion, lack of preparation, weak participation, or poor attendance. The board chair can head off a risky decision at the pass if the discussion seems to be going in that direction. While most motions can pass with a simple majority, the skilled chair knows that if there is a great divide among the board, a decision either way could continue to cause organizational strife. He or she will also be aware if the chief executive's position differs from the board majority's position and consider this fact when guiding the discussion. To reach consensus, the chair may choose to table the issue for a future meeting or assign further study to the chief executive and/or a board committee. The executive may also suggest alternative processes if he or she senses an impasse.

An experienced chief executive knows that it is important to leave board meetings with accountabilities clearly defined. The chief executive should clarify his or her role in the implementation of all board decisions and include a summary in the minutes. Or, if executing the decision is a little more involved, the chief executive might ask the board if he or she can work with a particular committee to see the project through. If there is any uncertainty, it is advisable to double-check with the chair rather than wait for the consequences.

There may be occasions when the board approves an action that the chief executive is not in favor of. Unless the action is illegal or unethical, the executive must implement it, but the process is negotiable. The chief executive can become more comfortable with the project by working through his or her concerns with the board chair, perhaps devising a more feasible mechanism for reaching the goal of the board decision.

SUPPORTING BOARD COMMITTEE WORK

Many boards handle their task-oriented work through committees or task forces, which engage board members in specific activities and maintain their involvement between board meetings. The chief executive should work closely with the chairs of these working groups and necessary staff to develop committee charges, job descriptions, and work plans that reflect the goals in the strategic plan. The executive can gain trust, intimacy, and feedback by bringing bigger-picture discussions to committee meetings instead of taking responsibility for the details of committee work.

For example, it is a standard practice of one human services organization that delivers meals to always set aside ample agenda time at committee meetings to discuss a catalytic question related to the overall health and well-being of the organization. For example, when a downturn in the economy negatively affected the organization's investment revenue, everyone's wisdom was tapped to brainstorm new funding sources and contacts in the community to help address the challenge. By involving board committees in discussion of this big-picture challenge, a successful social entrepreneurial catering business was formed at the organization, which is a complement to their nonprofit work in the community.

The chief executive and board chair have a special responsibility in providing orientation and ongoing support to committee and task force chairs. Volunteer and staff roles should be clearly defined, with the volunteer leadership providing overall direction and guidance to the committee's work as it relates to the mission of the organization, the strategic plan, and the committee's work plan. Volunteer leadership is also responsible for determining if a policy revision or addition can strengthen the work of the committee. This type of request should be brought to the board for discussion and consideration.

DETERMINING THE LEVEL OF STAFF SUPPORT

Organizations benefit from delegating staffing responsibility for committee work, since more can be accomplished when leadership is shared. As manager of the organization's staff, it is the chief executive's responsibility to facilitate staff–committee teamwork. Depending on the size and abilities of the staff and the types of committees that require support, the chief executive may designate other staff members to be the task-oriented communicators with board committees.

The board depends on the chief executive's judgment in choosing staff professionals to support at least some of the board's work. These staff members must understand that they do not work independently, but under the direction and message that the chief executive determines in concert with the board. A committee assignment is not an opportunity for a staff member to break loose and attempt to influence the organization's direction. Direction is the prerogative of the board and is communicated to staff through the chief executive.

Just as the chief executive and board chair should provide orientation and ongoing support to committee chairs, the chief executive should support staff members who are assigned to facilitate committee work. These staff members will find themselves in quicksand if they bring their personal task lists to committee meetings for discussion. An employee who asks committee members what should be served for lunch, what color napkins and tablecloths to order, or where to find phone numbers for donor prospects is inviting a committee to fall into an operational or staff role, which can lead to micromanagement and frustration on the part of both volunteers and staff. And it robs precious time that should be invested in a well-structured discussion that taps into the wisdom, contacts, and networks that board members bring to the table.

In evaluating whether a staff member is a good match with a board committee, the chief executive should consider these questions:

- Are the staff member's job responsibilities consistent with committee goals?

- Does the staff member have the experience and people skills to command the committee's respect?

- Does the staff member show a proper balance in allowing volunteer leaders to guide committee discussion, inserting his or her leadership when expertise or reining in is needed?

- Does the staff member (with the chief executive and committee chair) plan agendas that reflect the organization's strategic plan and work plan, well in advance of the meeting?

- Has the chief executive received positive feedback from board members and other committee members working with the staff member?

- Does the staff member understand that committee staffing authority is shared with the chief executive and that he or she should seek the chief executive's direction and advice in carrying out these duties?

- Does the staff member understand that he or she must share pertinent information from board members with the chief executive and that his or her organizational authority is limited to the committee goals?

The chief executive can coach the staff member in committee duties by reviewing draft meeting agendas before discussion with the committee chair, attending one or more committee meetings to observe the interaction, providing constructive feedback to the staff member, asking for feedback from the committee chair about the committee's progress, and monitoring the staff member's follow-up with the committee to ensure clarity of message, timeliness, and appropriate committee–staff division of responsibility.

BOARD CHAIR'S PERSPECTIVE

Getting all board members actively involved in the work of the mission is a huge challenge. Not all board members have the personality, comfort level, or internal drive to take the initiative to get involved. Some will wait to be asked for their help, invited to join a committee, or solicited for their input to a conversation — especially when seasoned board members or staff are perceived as experts.

It's important to remember the reasons why each board member was recruited and make sure the organization is benefiting from the expected offering. For example, if a board member has been chosen to broaden the diversity of the board, make sure that he or she feels welcomed. Don't expect the new member to be the sole spokesperson for his or her particular group — not all women have the same viewpoint, nor do all Latinos share a common perspective — but do ask if the person could offer thoughts on specific challenges. In one organization that I worked with, a new board member (who happened to be an ethnic minority) commented that a particular phrase being used to explain the organization's services could be misunderstood by some of its clients. With a minor wording change, the potentially troublesome term was replaced.

Looking for ways to involve new board members takes focus and care. While the chief executive has a vested interest in developing an environment that fosters full participation, it's a great opportunity to ask other board members to pair up with their new colleagues. Some organizations ask governance committee members to mentor new board members. In other cases, committee chairs or committee members check with the new members of their committees to ensure that they are assimilating with the group.

Special task forces or ad hoc committees are tremendous opportunities to engage the board and tap into their talents. Since the commitment is usually shorter or more defined than the work of a standing committee, board members who may be hesitant to engage in longer and more time-consuming activities might be willing to participate.

Here is an example of success: When I first became a board chair, I spearheaded the strategic planning review and truly wanted to gain the wisdom of all the talent of the organization. When we launched the endeavor, we took time at a board meeting to ask: "What has the organization been doing well?" and "What could we be doing better?" These two simple questions were a great way to get people talking. By breaking the large group into smaller groups, we encouraged participation. As each group summarized its discussion for the full board, they shared nuggets of new thought that might not have been offered in a larger group setting.

After a number of activities took place to gain additional input from all stakeholders, the board appointed an ad hoc committee to refine the materials and make final recommendations. This group included some of the organization's best thinkers. We also decided to add a few new folks to the mix: someone who had just joined the board, someone who frequently took opposing stands, and a younger committee member who was not on the board but had future board leadership potential. The dynamics of this group yielded a stronger product because of the new and diverse perspectives, and we gained advocates for the strategic plan.

Starting with the belief that each board member has time, talent, and treasure to offer our organization, our goal is to discover how to tap all three dimensions. We have found that it makes a difference when the board chair or the chief executive personally asks individual board members for their help.

VIEW FROM THE CHIEF EXECUTIVE'S DESK

I've learned through my years as a chief executive how important it is to structure the board's work around opening doors for the organization. Fundraising and donor development is most board members' number one fear. They need to understand that unless they "tell two friends, and those two friends tell two friends" the outlook for the organization is contraction, not expansion.

I guess it's human nature that when we try to mobilize board members to introduce the organization to their contacts, their immediate reactions are, "I don't like to ask for money" or "I don't know enough about this field to speak about it intelligently." These fears will stop most of them dead in their tracks unless the chief executive and board chair provide ongoing education, examples, and recognition for the value of opening doors.

At one board meeting each year, we host an outside speaker who addresses the value of board members in donor development. Role-playing the donor call is a key activity of this session. The development committee report highlights examples of board members who have been successful in making matches for the organization. For example, one of our board members recently changed jobs and within the first week in his new position, he researched his new company's involvement in community philanthropy. Within the next month, he arranged a meeting for me and the vice president in charge of charitable giving to talk about the organization. The board member attended the meeting and talked about his participation on the board, the level of involvement at his previous company, and why he believed the mission was important to his new company, its employees, and its customers. I filled in information about programs that had a direct impact on the company's employees and customers. The meeting ended with the vice president pledging involvement and financial support at the level that our board member suggested to him. This company had never contributed to our organization, but because one board member opened the door we have gained a major donor and volunteer participation.

PARTNERSHIP TIPS TO REMEMBER

- Keep your strategic plan alive by including its goals and key issues in board committee work plans, staff job descriptions, and in written progress reports at board meetings.

- Personally staff the nominating committee and facilitate recruitment of new members who are a good match with the organization's true needs.

- Work with the board chair to encourage board members and committee chairs to submit high-impact issues for board meeting discussion. Or, select a catalytic question from Appendix 2 (or develop one of your own) that is timely for your organization to open board discussion.

- Leave board meetings with accountabilities clearly defined.

- Consider delegating staff responsibility for selected committees of the board. More can be accomplished when leadership is shared.

- Alert the board chair to any information or issue that has the slightest chance of escalating into a risk for the organization. Your early warning and assessment will prepare the board to deal with the situation head on having the best chance at successful resolution.

- Work in partnership with the board chair (or development chair if there is one) to clarify each board member's responsibility and ability to open doors to needed resources. Together, make it clear that fundraising or resource development is a key component of board responsibilities.

CHAPTER 7
PLAN FOR TRANSITIONS

Lay the groundwork for changes in leadership .

One certainty in the lifecycle of a well-run, volunteer-driven organization is constant change. Organizations working toward best practice refresh and renew volunteer leadership on an ongoing basis. Bringing in "new blood" creates dynamism and fresh ideas and allows more tenured board members to move into positions of increased leadership.

Dramatic changes in chief executive positions are also on the horizon. The baby boomers are retiring at the same time that the nonprofit sector is growing. A 2006 study by The Bridgespan Group of nonprofit organizations with budgets of $250,000+ found that the nonprofit sector will need to attract and develop 640,000 new senior managers — the equivalent of 2.4 times the number currently employed. This is equivalent to recruiting over 50 percent of every MBA graduating class, at every college and university across the country, every year for the next 10 years.

Preparing for these inevitable transitions is critical in avoiding a disruption to the important work of the organization.

BOARD CHAIR TRANSITION

In an organization following the best practice of term limits for board members, the board chair position will change on a regular basis. For a chief executive, this is both a stressful and enriching opportunity. The stress can be managed and the enrichment increased with a clear plan in place that focuses on expectations and accountabilities in the chair–chief executive partnership.

MANAGING THE CHANGE OF THE BOARD CHAIR

A wise chief executive always considers the potential of each individual board member in relationship to moving up to the chair or other leadership positions. There are some board members who just rise to the surface as those with passion for the mission, an interest in all facets of the organization, a reliability and enthusiasm in their engagement in board and organizational activities, and an ability to communicate well and draw the best out of others. These are board members that the chief executive keeps an eye on and offers up to the nominating committee as good potentials for increased leadership in the organization.

This "farm system" for volunteer leadership benefits the chief executive, the volunteer, and ultimately the mission because it supports long-range planning that allows all parties to "try the shoes on" and determine their interest and level of commitment to move forward and upward in the volunteer leadership structure, including a path to the chair position.

Creating a chair-elect position as an intermediary step to moving into a board chair position is another way to prepare a volunteer leader to transition to board chair. Generally, the chair-elect will serve a one-year term in which he would shadow the chair in selected activities, sit in on committee meetings representing all facets of the organization, and meet regularly with the chief executive and sitting chair to get updates on the key challenges facing the organization and progress on the strategic plan. This type of immersion in the business of the organization can help create a well-prepared new board chair that is practiced in his partnership with the chief executive and can make a smooth transition into his new role.

It is also important that the current chair and chief executive talk with the board chair candidate about the realistic time commitment one must make to be an engaged and informed board chair. Add up the time in an average month that encompasses the key functions of a board chair and what your organization needs and expects. Include responsibilities like the following:

- Board meetings — preplanning, attendance, follow-up

- Committee meetings — most chairs serve as an ex-officio member of all committees and attend at least one meeting of each annually

- Special events and fundraisers — most chairs will want to attend most of these to model participative behavior for the rest of the board and show support to the staff and volunteers responsible for leading the event

- Regular conferences with the chief executive — to get updates on all facets of the organization and work together in addressing challenges

- Homework — written or electronic information important to the business operation of the organization including financial statements, some committee reports, newsletters, etc.

Eager to fill the spot, sometimes a recruitment strategy going something like this is used: "This position will take hardly any of your time.... The staff does everything and you run the meetings." This may get you a board chair candidate, but it rarely gets the organization what it needs from a leader. It is unimaginable that chief executive candidates would be recruited on this premise, so expecting different results from a board chair candidate will likely prove to be disappointing.

The "quick sell" recruitment does little to prepare a mind-set of partnership and accountability in minding the organization's current business and shaping its future. A board position undersold is likely to result in poor transition, an underperforming board chair, and a frustrating partnership with the chief executive.

WHEN LIFE'S LITTLE SURPRISES HAPPEN

Even the best laid plans to allow for a smooth transition to the board chair spot can be altered by the surprises that life brings. Your board chair could resign, be transferred out of your area, become ill, or even worse. The same situations can apply to your chair-elect. Or, during the time that the chair-elect is exposed to the organization, he may decide that the job is not his cup of tea and forgo moving to the chair slot.

Certainly vacancies in key leadership positions are not uncommon to chief executives in nonprofit organizations. However, it should not be uncommon to have a plan and process in place to fill a vacancy in the chief volunteer position expeditiously with the best candidate for the job.

Many organizations have bylaws that specifically designate the board officer position that becomes the automatic nominee to the chair slot. This might be the chair-elect or a vice chair. Other organizations leave more of their options open by avoiding the automatic "monkey move up" and looking to a wider range of possibilities including the immediate past chair, the secretary, the former usual suspects, or another seasoned board member who is the best candidate to provide leadership for the organization's current situation and needs.

> *A board position undersold is likely to result in poor transition, an underperforming board chair, and a frustrating partnership with the chief executive.*

In the case of an unplanned vacancy in the chair position, the candidate elected to fill the spot may only agree to do so on a shorter-term basis rather than for a regular term of one or more years. This gives the chief executive and board time to recruit and groom a longer-term replacement.

CHIEF EXECUTIVE TRANSITIONS

Most of the reasons for a departure of the chief executive — resignation, termination, illness, or death — do not allow for the luxury of considerable planning once announced. However, unless the chief executive is immortal, her departure is inevitable — sooner or later. A good chief executive brings the issue of succession planning to light for her board and works with it on a realistic preparedness plan that fits the organization and supports its mission.

According to a 2006 study by The Bridgespan Group, the charitable sector will be increasingly drawn into an all-out "war for talent" with the government and business sectors. The same study reports that the number of 35- to 44-year-olds in the United States will decline between 2000 and 2015 even as the demand for new nonprofit executives continues to grow. The study predicts that by 2016 the nonprofit sector will need 80,000 new senior managers each year, 40 percent more each year than is currently required.

While no chief executive wants to think she may become too old to lead the organization or even die, the challenge is clear — it is imperative to consider leadership transition as a critical responsibility of the chief executive's job.

At a 2010 American Institute of CPA's Not-For-Profit Financial Executive Forum, Jeanne Bell, CEO of CompassPoint Nonprofit Services, said the sector suffers not from a leadership deficit but from a dearth of intentional leadership development.

Bell offered a series of observations she has gathered from several sources that reflect the state of nonprofit succession planning:

- The notion of "leadership" is in as much transition as our leaders are.

- It is difficult to advance people in an organization if the people leading it are not willing to give up their control, delegate, and get people involved.

- Most nonprofits are a puzzle put together in a darkened room. Eight out of ten pieces are in the wrong place. That is, eight out of ten employees feel miscast.

- Strength is talent multiplied by both knowledge (which is factual and experiential) and skills (accumulated knowledge in a sequence of steps leading to performance).

- Talents are recurring patterns of thought, feeling, or behavior that can be applied productively.

Most organizations do not have the resources to bring an "executive in training" on staff to learn the ropes and serve as the "maiden in waiting." Still, all organizations have the capacity to have well-thought-out and documented succession resources that can be put into play if the chief executive position is vacant. Some examples are

- Hire people to fill more senior or manager positions that are less technically skilled and more generalist-experienced wherever possible. Develop these generalists by exposing them to all aspects of the organization. Not only does the organization develop people who can be useful in multiple ways, chances are improved that at least one or more emerging leaders could serve as an interim chief executive or solid candidate to fill the slot permanently.

- Maintain relationships with retired nonprofit leaders, consultants and nonprofit federations that can supply interim leaders or permanent candidates.

- Organizations with state, regional, or national offices can turn to this resource for interim staffing and help with an executive search beginning with their own "farm system" of potential candidates for the job.

- Keep a list of past board members and staff who can be called upon for help to fill in or have networks of contacts to help in the search for a replacement. Good ways to keep talented and committed past board and staff members involved include honorary board membership, committee memberships, and regular informal networking.

- Maintain a strong strategic plan that can provide the basics for a leadership agenda — organization vision, strategic direction, systems improvements, and board development needs. A leadership agenda is used in the executive search process to craft a candidate profile that includes the experience, skills, and characteristics of an incoming chief executive to successfully pursue the strategic goals in the leadership agenda.

Succession planning is much more than having talent on tap to fill the chief executive's spot in the event of vacancy. BoardSource's *Chief Executive Succession Planning: Essential Guidance for Boards and CEOs, Second Edition,* by Nancy Axelrod, approaches succession planning as an ongoing and adaptive process rather than a specific event. By guiding and supporting best practices for sound governance and organization operations, the chief executive has already done much of what is required for successful executive transition.

> *A good chief executive brings the issue of succession planning to light for her board and works with it on a realistic preparedness plan that fits the organization and supports its mission.*

Axelrod details the practices that are important in the succession planning cycle. These are all areas of attention that the chief executive can initiate or support:

- **Understanding the job of the nonprofit chief executive** — a board that understands the unique challenges of nonprofit leadership and the type of individual best suited to the job is a board that will make the best choices when it comes to short- and long-term solutions to bridging the gap in staff leadership.

- **Developing an emergency transition plan** — a board that understands how organizational functions of greatest concern will be handled during an emergency transition — communications, financial oversight, interim management, and executive search — and makes sure that this information is documented and accessible.

- **Agreeing on expectations** — the board defines mutual expectations of the chief executive and the board.

- **Establishing evaluation process for chief executive** — an established process is supported by an up-to-date job description and annual goals.

- **Conducting board self-assessment** — the board looks at its own performance, knows what it wants from its members and makes continuous improvements.

See Appendix 12 for Axelrod's Chief Executive Succession Plan Guidelines.

Having a plan in place and resources to turn to when either the board chair or chief executive position vacates allows the organization to keep the focus on the mission versus the crisis of leadership. It also shows forethought on the part of the board and outgoing chief executive that translates into a sense of security and a minimization of the anxiety and inertia that can result when a plan is not in place and the process to replace the chief executive is unknown to the key stakeholders.

BoardSource offers a collection of books designed to help create a proactive succession plan, hire and support a new chief executive, and establish an effective compensation structure:

Chief Executive Succession Planning: Essential Guidance for Boards and CEOs, Second Edition, helps create a well-thought-out plan that starts well before the hiring process.

Chief Executive Transitions: How to Hire and Support a Nonprofit CEO helps to navigate the hiring process and oversee a successful leadership transition.

Nonprofit Executive Compensation: Planning, Performance, and Pay, Second Edition, helps organizations maintain public trust by increasing transparency and integrity of compensation practices.

VIEW FROM THE BOARD CHAIR

Having a strategy for how to address filling key roles in the organization takes a careful and deliberate focus. When I am filling the role of board chair, my concern for protecting the organization in terms of its human assets causes me to consider both the chief executive and the board chair positions. An unplanned vacancy in either of these key roles can have a devastating impact and yet such openings occur much too often.

For the chief executive role, most organizations that I have supported have had "lean" staffs. Many of the key internal leaders who are direct reports to the chief executive have terrific functional knowledge in one or two areas. Rarely do they have broad "leadership of the entire organization" in their skill package — maybe the ability to learn but the learning would be "on the job." Where possible, it's important to give talented subordinates the chance to broaden their experiences. Giving such leaders a special assignment from time to time will help develop their general management skills.

For organizations that are simply too small to ever develop potential chief executives, it's important for the current chief executive and the board chair to have a serious discussion about how the entity could manage through this void of leadership. The wise chief executive does not feel intimidated by this discussion but rather demonstrates his care for the organization, the staff, the board, and all the various individuals who would be impacted.

Equally important is the need to find one's replacement — unless being the permanent board chair is one's goal! In each case, I am eager to identify someone to fill a vice chair position (or similar role) as early as possible so I can start involving that individual in critical discussions of a strategic nature. For example, in one organization where I am board chair, the vice chair has helped plan the upcoming board retreat. Together we have identified the requisite board talents needed as new members are identified. This involvement will serve both the soon-to-be board chair and the organization — and will make the upcoming transition seamless.

I have also found that some individuals who would be excellent board chairs are hesitant to consider stepping into this role since they see their own "flaws" and question whether they have all the skills needed. In one situation, the individual was not a comfortable public speaker — something that I did relatively well. In recruiting him for the leadership role he confessed his major concern for this part of the job. I reminded him that each of the many board chairs that our organization had been fortunate to have all had different strengths. While the chief executive had to adjust the approach to the "public speaking" that the new board chair did — and gradually gave him small pieces to build his confidence, other board members were tapped to play enhanced roles. Being flexible and working with the abilities — not focusing on the weaknesses — and by taking a fresh look at how things were done, the chief executive enabled this shy leader to be successful.

VIEW FROM THE CHIEF EXECUTIVE'S DESK

Over the course of my nonprofit chief executive career, I've worked in partnership with 15 different board chairs and groomed an additional four that were recruited for the position but left midterm due to a move from our service area.

Probably the most emotionally challenging aspect of these changes in partnerships is that a very strong professional bond must be formed rather quickly and transitioned just as quickly. I've had my favorites over the years — those that brought great benefits to the organization and cared about developing my skills and opportunities for growth. Sometimes the partnership really clicked in a way that I hadn't expected and I've felt a sense of personal loss transitioning this gratifying relationship to move on to the next.

To reduce this anxiety and allow for a smooth transition that is helpful to both me and the new board chair, my organization designated an officer position for the outgoing board chair — immediate past chair — which allows continued participation on our board in a slot where he can continue to train and support me and the new board chair. I have found that the immediate past chair can pass on a sense of the culture of the board chair–chief executive relationship and help our new partnership be as successful as it can be right from the start.

Another occasional challenge I've had with an incoming board chair is a lack of understanding that a chair role, by its nature, requires that they invest their time and talents to "get the best from the board." There have been a few chairs and chair-elects that have gravitated toward "managing the chief executive and the staff" or in treating the members of the board in ways they would treat subordinates on the job. I have always been thankful for the transition time period that has allowed for important conversations to take place about staff and board roles prior to a chair moving into the spot for his term.

I have found it always works best to discuss roles, responsibilities, and accountabilities at the recruitment meeting and continue if there is a hint of concern as the process toward assuming the chair role moves along.

When I've found challenge or resistance in reaching a successful outcome in these corrective conversations, I have found it helpful to get advice and insight from seasoned board members before moving forward in further development of the partnership with the incoming board chair. Not only have these advisors provided sound counsel to me in how I can improve, they can also be helpful to an incoming chair by providing useful feedback from a peer perspective.

Over the years, there have been a few board chair candidates who have stepped aside after they had experienced the role by shadowing the current chair or by actively participating in a diverse variety of organizational activities and functions of which the board chair needs to have some working knowledge to do the job well.

Certainly I would not recommend recruiting a board chair before having a discussion about expectations. But, sometimes moving board members from roles where they have performed effectively as a special event or standing committee chairs to roles of big-picture leadership with the organization turns out to be a difficult fit, even with upfront information about what is expected of a board chair. It is in these situations that I have recognized the value of helping the board fill the leadership pipeline with a diverse group of emerging leaders and insisting that the chair-elect slot be taken seriously.

PARTNERSHIP TIPS TO REMEMBER

- Develop a volunteer leadership pipeline by keeping an eye on talented and reliable board members who can be moved to positions of increasing responsibility.

- Create a chair-elect position as an intermediary step to moving into your board chair role. Use this time to immerse him in all aspects of your organization and enhance your partnership in caring for your organization as a team.

- Be honest and specific about the time commitment necessary for a board chair to be successful at the job.

- Always have more than one board member cued up to assume your board chair role. Unexpected things can happen and having options will help your organization move forward with fewer bumps in the road. And in times of crisis, the prior board chair often may be willing to provide leadership until a more permanent selection can be made.

- Consider a permanent officer position on the board for your immediate past board chair to ease the transition of board leadership bridging the past to the present and helping the chief executive and incoming board chair forge their relationship.

- Present the topic of chief executive succession planning to your board and help it to develop a realistic preparedness plan that fits your organization and supports the mission.

- Groom senior staff and keep in regular touch with selected past staff and board members who have the skills and experience to fill in when a chief executive vacancy occurs or can serve as a qualified candidate for filling the position permanently.

CONCLUSION

Being a constructive partner to the board is conceivably the most critical role a chief executive plays. The chief executive's own professional success, as well as the success of the organization at carrying out its mission, depends on this strong and effective partnership. Throughout these pages we've shared ideas to help move the partnership with the board from good to great. But perhaps the most important advice that we can offer is to trust what you already know and to continually work to gain new knowledge and wisdom.

Chief executives are people, too. They have experienced relationships of all types throughout their lives, and they've learned to recognize cues that signal when a relationship is or isn't thriving. The executive who recognizes that his or her relationship with the board is similar to a relationship with a spouse, a significant other, or a friend, can put that life experience to work and either enrich the partnership or change direction to increase the likelihood of success.

While the chief executive may not kiss board members goodnight or ask them to pick up their dirty laundry, the components of a meaningful, successful partnership with the board sound a lot like a self-help book:

- Know yourself, accept who you are, and always work to improve. Be 100 percent genuine.

- Think of your board in a positive light — like a friend or a treasure just waiting for your help to make the most of its gifts.

- Structure time with individual board members, small groups, and the whole board. Concentrate on seeking a quality outcome for the time spent.

- Be thoughtful about what you communicate, how, when, and where, but always keep the lines open.

- Set goals for the relationship with the board. Ask yourself each day what you can do to grow and enrich the relationship. Complete at least one action daily that is focused on deepening it.

- Accept responsibility and ownership for the work that the board expects from you.

- Be constantly aware of what your board needs from you, and be up front about what you need from it. Clarify, negotiate, and deliver.

- Embrace the changes that come with a new board chair, ever-changing board composition, and the competing interests that come with both. Change is inevitable and provides opportunities for fresh ideas and growth.

- If you take any action to enhance your relationship with the board, expect missteps and failures. These life lessons contribute to your continued growth, and you can learn from them and turn them into positives in the future.

Our hope is that this book will build on what you already know, and cause you to reflect on, re-examine, reinforce, or reshape your approaches to building a relationship with your board.

APPENDIX 1
BOARD MEMBER EXPECTATIONS FOR XYZ ORGANIZATION

1. Agree to serve a three-year term and successfully complete responsibilities outlined in the job description, in partnership with staff liaison.

2. Commit an average of six to 10 hours monthly to fulfilling your job responsibilities.

3. Attend and actively participate in required meetings.

4. Serve on one standing or other leadership committee and attend its regular meetings.

5. Attend [volunteer orientation session].

6. Understand the organization's mission and be willing to promote the organization in light of the mission.

7. Contribute financially at a meaningful level within your own means.

8. Schedule a planned giving visit with our director of development or planned giving consultant to discuss your plans for leaving a legacy to the organization and other charitable causes.

9. Participate in at least one special event as a sponsor, participant, attendee, or volunteer.

10. Observe or participate in one community service program annually.

11. Have fun, learn, teach, and share in successes and failures. Provide honest, constructive feedback to benefit the success of the organization.

Signed: _____ Date: _____

APPENDIX 2
CATALYTIC QUESTIONS

In *Governance as Leadership: Reframing the Work of Nonprofit Boards*, authors Richard P. Chait, William P. Ryan, and Barbara Taylor suggest posing catalytic questions to nonprofit boards that invite creativity and exploration, and do not depend largely on data and logic to answer:

- What three adjectives or short phrases best characterize this organization?

- What will be most strikingly different about this organization in five years?

- What do you hope will be most strikingly different about this organization in five years?

- On what list, which you could create, would you like this organization to rank at the top?

- Five years from today, what will this organization's key constituents consider the most important legacy of the current board?

- What will be most different about the board or how we govern in five years?

- How would we respond if a donor offered a $50 million endowment to the one organization in our field that had the best idea for becoming a more valuable public asset?

- How would we look as a take-over target by a potential or actual competitor?

- If we could successfully take over another organization, which one would we choose and why?

- What has a competitor done successfully that we would not choose to do as a matter of principle?

- What have we done that a competitor might not do as a matter of principle?

- What headline would we most/least like to see about the organization?

- What is the biggest gap between what the organization claims it is and what it actually is?

APPENDIX 3
SAMPLE BOARD CHAIR PLATFORM

Encourage new board chairs to consider what special focus they would like to have for the organization. This focus is something that they want to accomplish during their tenure. The following examples are among those that several different board chairs employed during their time as board chair of a public health organization. This exercise should not replace or undo any of the organization's agreed-upon strategic goals, but may be helpful in terms of prioritizing them.

- Build greater board engagement.

- Show how board involvement makes a difference to the organization in advocacy, collaboration, and cooperation.

- Build a closer relationship with the national organization.

- Reward accomplishments in diversity.

- Preserve and protect the organization's government granting agency.

- Position the organization as a key player in the public health arena through inter-organizational collaboration and partnerships.

- Focus on partnerships with organizations on aging to build mission and funding relationships.

APPENDIX 4
SAMPLE COMMUNICATIONS AND ACCOUNTABILITY PACT

By agreeing to how each leader will interact with his or her counterpart (chief executive and board chair), communications expectations are discussed up front. These may be a good starting point for your own organization. But be sure to craft commitments that work for your particular needs!

The chief executive will

- Share both good news and bad news immediately.

- Provide time for weekly telephone and monthly in-person updates.

- Alert the board chair to any information or issue that has the slightest chance of escalating into a risk for the organization.

Add your own here:

The board chair will

- Make time to develop the agenda of each board meeting in concert with the chief executive.

- Provide honest feedback to the chief executive in regard to the purview of his or her responsibilities and performance.

- Develop a platform of issues in concert with the chief executive to be advanced during his or her term.

- Be timely and responsive to the requests of the chief executive, recognizing that at least in some instances, it is not appropriate for the chief executive to determine organizational direction or response without participation of the governing body.

Add your own here:

APPENDIX 5
BASIC RESPONSIBILITIES OF THE BOARD AND CHIEF EXECUTIVE

TEN BASIC RESPONSIBILITIES OF NONPROFIT BOARDS

1. Determine mission and purpose. It is the board's responsibility to create and review a statement of mission and purpose that articulates the organization's goals, means, and primary constituents served.

2. Select the chief executive. Boards must reach consensus on the chief executive's responsibilities and undertake a careful search to find the most qualified individual for the position.

3. Support and evaluate the chief executive. The board should ensure that the chief executive has the moral and professional support he or she needs to further the goals of the organization.

4. Ensure effective planning. Boards must actively participate in an overall planning process and assist in implementing and monitoring the plan's goals.

5. Monitor, and strengthen programs and services. The board's responsibility is to determine which programs are consistent with the organization's mission and monitor their effectiveness.

6. Ensure adequate financial resources. One of the board's foremost responsibilities is to secure adequate resources for the organization to fulfill its mission.

7. Protect assets and provide proper financial oversight. The board must assist in developing the annual budget and ensuring that proper financial controls are in place.

8. Build a competent board. All boards have a responsibility to articulate prerequisites for candidates, orient new members, and periodically and comprehensively evaluate their own performance.

9. Ensure legal and ethical integrity. The board is ultimately responsible for adherence to legal standards and ethical norms.

10. Enhance the organization's public standing. The board should clearly articulate the organization's mission, accomplishments, and goals to the public and garner support from the community.

Source: Richard T. Ingram, Ten Basic Responsibilities of Nonprofit Boards, Second Edition (BoardSource, 2009).

THE NONPROFIT CHIEF EXECUTIVE'S TEN BASIC RESPONSIBILITIES

1. Commit to the mission.

2. Lead the staff and manage the organization.

3. Exercise responsible financial stewardship.

4. Lead and manage fundraising.

5. Follow the highest ethical standards, ensure accountability, and comply with the law.

6. Engage the board in planning and lead implementation.

7. Develop future leadership.

8. Build external relationships and serve as an advocate.

9. Ensure the quality and effectiveness of programs.

10. Support the board.

Source: Richard L. Moyers, The Nonprofit Chief Executive's Ten Basic Responsibilities *(BoardSource, 2006).*

APPENDIX 6
BOARD PERFORMANCE REPORT CARD

The results of BoardSource's *Nonprofit Governance Index 2010,* conducted in June 2010, show that while many nonprofits have put the critical components of good governance in place, much room for improvement remains.

Use the following format to develop a board performance report card for your organization. Have each board member grade the board's performance in the areas below. After averaging their grades use the report card as a way to spark discussion by benchmarking your board's grades to those of all chief executives and board members participating in the nationwide survey. Use the sample questions as discussion starters. Action items can be developed where improvement is desired or longer-term improvements can be integrated into the strategic plan.

Prepare for this exercise by reviewing the entire survey at www.boardsource.org and search by "BoardSource *Nonprofit Governance Index 2010.*"

Board Performance Report Card	Your Board	Benchmark All Board Members*	Benchmark All Chief Executives**
Understanding the organization's mission		B+	B+
Financial oversight		B+	B+
Legal and ethical oversight		B	B
Knowledge of the organization's programs		C+	B+
Providing guidance and support to the chief executive		C+	B+
Level of commitment and involvement		C+	B
Evaluating the chief executive		C+	B
Strategic planning and thinking		C+	B
Monitoring organizational performance		C+	C+
Understanding board's roles and responsibilities		C+	B
Recruiting new board members		C+	C+
Community relations and outreach		C	C+
Increasing board diversity		C	C+
Fundraising		D+	C+

* Board members' self evaluation
** Chief executive evaluation of their boards

Sample questions:

What are the two most pressing challenges confronting nonprofit organizations?

Survey results: financial stability, board development/engagement

What are the top eight most important areas for board improvement?

Survey results:

1. Fundraising

2. Strategic planning

3. Focus (more strategic, less operational)

4. Board composition and diversity

5. Board members commitment, engagement, attendance

6. Board self-assessment

7. Board recruitment

8. Board development/orientation

How much should board members give?

Survey results: It is common practice that the first measure of board giving should be 100 percent participation, and the second is the expectation of a personally significant or stretch gift for all board members. Seventy-one percent of all board members whose organizations engage in fundraising, make a personal contribution.

APPENDIX 7

SAMPLE BOARD OF DIRECTORS' PERFORMANCE MATRIX

For this organization, four key board responsibilities have been identified and behavioral statements help clarify the different levels of participation. For many board members who have a competitive spirit to "be the best," this spurs enhanced outcomes.

Each member of the board plays a key role in the success of this organization, both in terms of governance and support. It is recognized that each member has a unique and valued set of attributes in terms of time, talent, and treasure to assist in achieving our mission and vision. To serve on this board is both a responsibility and a privilege. This matrix is intended to provide a benchmarking tool for board members to evaluate their level of contribution in the various aspects of their board responsibilities.

Board Member Function	Threshold Participation	Full Participation	Exceptional Participation
Board/Committe Meetings	• Attend at least 70% of meetings and actively participate/provide input • Read/understand all material provided for meetings • Participate on a board committee	• Meet Threshold expectations • Attend 85% of meetings	• Meet Full expectations • Serve as a committee chair or an officer of the board
Stewardship of Talent and Treasure (Includes In-kind)	• Personally make annual contribution • Leverage gifts/in-kind contributions	• Meet Threshold expectations • Contribute to and attend at least one fundraising event • Identify and solicit financial contributions and participation in organization fundraising from others	• Meet Full expectations • Contribute to and attend more than one fundraising event • Help identify new sources of revenue • Provide professional expertise for the organization operations

Board Member Function	Threshold Participation	Full Participation	Exceptional Participation
Board Development	• Attend board orientation sessions • Understand and articulate mission vision and key service offerings • Provide names of potential board candidates	• Meet Threshold expectations • Nominate candidate(s) who can contribute to the organization	• Meet Full expectations • Actively recruit candidate(s) • Mentor new board members
Enhance Organization's Public Standing	• Become familiar with programs and services offered • Clearly articulate the mission, vision, programs/services, accomplishments, and goals within one's own sphere of influence	• Meet Threshold expectations • Speak with others outside organization about mission, goals, accomplishments and needs	• Meet Full expectations • Actively garner support from the community • Attend community events/meetings on behalf of the organization and promote organization to others

APPENDIX 8
SAMPLE ANNUAL LEADERSHIP SURVEY

Each year this organization polls its board members to identify those who are satisfied with their board service and those who may wish to make changes.

XYZ Organization greatly values your service as a member of the board of directors. The success of the organization depends upon an actively engaged and committed board of directors. To achieve this end, the governance committee would like to hear your thoughts and feedback relative to the following. We will consider your feedback as we launch our volunteer leadership assessment and recruitment process for the coming year.

Name:

1. I am interested in continuing to serve on the board of directors.

    Yes   No   Maybe, depending on:

_____

_____

_____

2. The most valuable contribution(s) I can make to XYZ Organization is/are:

_____

_____

_____

3. Rate your level of satisfaction with your service on the board.

    (5=high satisfaction, 1=low satisfaction):

4. How, do you believe, can your level of satisfaction with board service be increased?

_____

_____

_____

5. What obstacles have you encountered in achieving active, satisfying board participation?

_____

_____

_____

6. I am committed to making an annual financial contribution to XYZ.

   Yes   No

7. I am willing to solicit support from others for XYZ Organization's mission.

   Yes (Name prospects you are willing to call on, and explain what type of assistance prospect(s) can offer.)

_____

_____

   No

8. I currently serve on the following board committees:

_____

_____

_____

9. I would like to continue to serve on the same committees in the same capacity in the coming year.

   Yes

   No (If no, please indicate where/how you would like to serve.)

_____

_____

10. I am interested in serving as a board officer now or in the future.

    Yes   No

11. I am interested in learning how to work my way up to the chair position in the future.

    Yes   No

Other comments:

APPENDIX 9
SAMPLE BOARD MEMBER PROFILE

1. Name: _____

   Title: _____

   Company: _____

   Business Address: _____

   City: _____ State: _____ ZIP: _____

   Telephone: _____ Fax: _____

   Home Address: _____

   City: _____ State: _____ ZIP: _____

   Telephone: _____

   E-mail: _____

   Cell phone: _____

2. Previous involvement with XYZ Organization:

   _____

   _____

   _____

3. Other philanthropic, charitable, and community involvement:

   _____

   _____

   _____

4. I believe that I can commit _____ hours/month to XYZ Organization work.

5. I believe that I can recruit _____ hours/month in additional volunteer service support from family and/or co-workers.

6. I am committed to making a meaningful annual financial contribution to XYZ Organization within my own means.

   Yes   No

7. I am willing to solicit financial support from others for XYZ Organization's mission.

    Yes   No

8. I am willing to consider a planned gift to XYZ Organization.

    Yes   No

    If yes: now   in the future

9. I have the level of control over my time and schedule that will allow me to attend all required XYZ Organization meetings if I am given advance notice of the dates (e.g., two months' notice).

    Yes   No

10. I rate my ability to provide the following resources (10=high, 1=low):

    Financial support:

    Explain:

    _____

    _____

    People to help:

    Explain:

    _____

    _____

    Expertise:

    Explain:

    _____

    _____

    Contacts that can help XYZ:

    Explain:

    _____

    _____

    In-kind services/products:

    Explain:

    _____

    _____

11. Additional comments or questions:

APPENDIX 10
SAMPLE ANNUAL SCORE CARD

Challenges	Goals	Actions
Increase in stray cats	Increase # cats rescued by 20% per year	• Hire two new staff for rescue team • Add to facility to house more cats
City eliminated animal shelter	Merge with similar organization	• Research possible merger partners • Determine benefits of merger • Hold at least one exploratory meeting
More cats rescued are sick	Secure donated vet services	• Contact local vet school • Form alliance with Vet Association
City grant will run out in two years	Implement first special event	• Determine event • Recruit chair • Set budget • Execute

APPENDIX 11
SAMPLE BOARD OF DIRECTORS MEETING FEEDBACK FORM

Use this form is to evaluate overall effectiveness of this board meeting process. Please rank the following items on a scale of 1–5 using a "1" when your expectations are not met and a "5" when your expectations are exceeded. We will use your feedback to make modifications to make our board meetings high-impact and get the best we can from our board!

	Exceeds Expectations		Meets Expectations		Below Expectations
1. The agenda supports the mission of our organization.	5	4	3	2	1
2. Meeting materials were provided to all board members in a timely manner.	5	4	3	2	1
3. Materials prepared me to participate in the meeting.	5	4	3	2	1
4. The agenda utilized my time and skills appropriate to my role and responsibilities as a board member.	5	4	3	2	1
5. Discussions focused on strategy and policy levels, not operational.	5	4	3	2	1
6. Appropriate board and staff assignments were made.	5	4	3	2	1
7. Meeting goals were met.	5	4	3	2	1
8. Meeting start and end were on time.	5	4	3	2	1

Please provide further feedback here:

_____

_____

_____

_____

Suggested agenda topics for future meetings:

_____

_____

_____

_____

APPENDIX 12
CHIEF EXECUTIVE SUCCESSION PLAN GUIDELINES

Succession planning can strategically position an organization for success before an expected or unforeseen departure of the chief executive. There is no generic template for executive succession planning that will apply to every organization. While the content and timeline of the succession plan should be customized to the circumstances and culture of each organization, the following practices reflect an effective plan.

On an annual basis:

- Create or update an emergency leadership transition plan.

- Conduct a performance review of the chief executive.

- Assess the chief executive performance against mutually agreed-upon goals and expectations determined the previous year.

- Implement a process for reviewing the compensation of the chief executive that conforms to the IRS Form 990 and best practice requirements.

- Determine institutional goals and personal goals that the chief executive will be accountable for during the next performance assessment process.

- Clarify expectations between the board and chief executive.

- Ensure that the board and the chief executive have shared goals and a collective vision of how the organization should be evolving over the next three to five years.

- Discussion the chief executive's future plans (regarding term of office).

- Review or update the chief executive job description.

- Determine whether the succession plan should be created, updated, or tweaked.

- Conduct a board self-assessment.

- Identify the board's strengths and needs.

- Define goals that the board is responsible for implementing.

- Determine how well the board is working with the chief executive.

- Determine actions the board will take to act on the results of the board self-assessment for the purpose of strengthening its structure and practices.

When the chief executive's departure is known:

- Implement emergency leadership transition actions, if necessary.

- Discuss lessons learned by board and staff members who participated in the last chief executive transition process that represent things to repeat or avoid during the next transition.

- Create a schedule for the executive transition.

- Communicate the executive transition plan with the appropriate constituencies.

- Conduct an organizational assessment to determine leadership needs relevant for next chief executive.

- Convene a search committee to create chief executive profile, recruit candidates, rank applicants, interview candidates, check references, and recommend final candidate(s) to the board.

- Select a new chief executive,

After the new chief executive is selected:

- Create a leadership transition team.

- Implement a communications plan to inform the community of the new appointment.

- Provide a formal orientation for the new chief executive.

- Agree on written goals ad expectations for the chief executive.

- Ensure that the expectations and decision-making responsibilities between the board and the chief executive are well delineated.

- Create a timeline for a new succession plan (which defines the role of the board and the chief executive in the process).

Source: Nancy R. Axelrod, Chief Executive Succession Planning: Essential Guidance for Boards and CEOs, Second Edition *(BoardSource 2010).*

SUGGESTED RESOURCES

Axelrod, Nancy R. *Chief Executive Succession Planning: Essential Guidance for Boards and CEOs, Second Edition.* Washington, DC: BoardSource, 2011.
Chief executive succession planning is not only about determining your organization's next leader. It is a continuous process that assesses your organization's needs and identifies leadership that supports those needs. A successful succession plan is linked to the strategic plan, mission, and vision. Author Nancy Axelrod helps board members prepare for the future by examining the ongoing and intermittent steps of executive succession planning.

BoardSource. *The Source: Twelve Principles of Governance That Power Exceptional Boards.* Washington, DC: BoardSource, 2005.
Exceptional boards add significant value to their organizations, making discernible differences in their advance on mission. *The Source* defines governance not as dry, obligatory compliance, but as a creative and collaborative process that supports chief executives, engages board members, and furthers the causes they all serve. Aspirational in nature, these principles offer chief executives a description of an empowered board that is a strategic asset to be leveraged, and provide board members with a vision of what is possible and a way to add lasting value to the organizations they lead.

Carlson, Mim and Margaret Donohoe. *The Executive Director's Survival Guide: Thriving as a Nonprofit Leader.* San Francisco: Jossey-Bass, 2002.
This resource provides new insight, inspiration, and tools to meet the real-life challenges and rewards of leading a nonprofit organization, and to thrive in this big job. Written by experienced nonprofit professionals and consultants on nonprofit leadership, the book gives the help chief executives need to develop and strengthen personal, interpersonal, and organizational effectiveness. It is filled with practical advice for succeeding in the position and offers a reader-friendly question-and-answer format.

Chait, Richard P., William P. Ryan, and Barbara E. Taylor. *Governance as Leadership: Reframing the Work of Nonprofit Boards.* Hoboken, NJ: John Wiley & Sons and Washington, DC: BoardSource, 2005.
Governance as Leadership introduces a fresh way to think about governance, with sensible guidance to turn these ideas into concrete actions. It is based on new thinking: that nonprofit managers have become leaders; board members are acting more like managers; there are three equal modes of governance — fiduciary, strategic, generative — and three modes are better than two or one.

Dambach, Charles F., Melissa Davis, and Robert L. Gale. *Structures and Practices of Nonprofit Boards, Second Edition*. Washington, DC: BoardSource, 2009.
Looking for ways to improve efficiency? Help your board members keep long-term goals and board development at the forefront of their work. Included are practical guidelines on structural issues, such as running meetings, committee structure, size of the board, and term limits. Improve the way that your board works by increasing flexibility and improving interpersonal relationships.

Flynn, Outi. *Meeting, and Exceeding Expectations: A Guide to Successful Nonprofit Board Meetings, Second Edition*. Washington, DC: BoardSource, 2009.
Whether you're new to the boardroom or an old pro, you'll find ready-to-use information in this resource. Based on actual meeting observations, this book will provide you with practical solutions to better meetings, explanation of the legal framework, and process practices that will reinvigorate your board meetings. With a detailed table of contents, this book is a must-have reference guide for nonprofit chief executives, board members, senior staff, and any other participant in key meetings of the board.

Grace, Kay Sprinkel, Amy McClellan, and John A. Yankey. *The Nonprofit Board's Role in Mission, Planning, and Evaluation, Second Edition*. Washington, DC: BoardSource, 2009.
All too often, nonprofit boards look at mission, planning, and evaluation in isolation. This book, however, offers an integrated approach. A regular and consistent planning process helps the board and staff clarify mission and make changes when necessary to keep mission fresh, lively, and relevant. A systematic evaluation process generates information to help formulate goals and provide the framework for measuring those goals against mission.

Howe, Fisher. *The Nonprofit Leadership Team: Building the Board-Executive Director Partnership*. San Francisco: Jossey-Bass, 2003.
This resource focuses on the key leadership team — the board, its chair, and the chief executive — and shows how they can work in partnership to lead an effective, healthy organization. The text covers every aspect of leading an organization as a team, clearly showing what the board expects of the executive and what the executive expects of the board and the individual members, examining the working relationship among them, and demonstrating how the leadership team deals with specific responsibilities and challenges.

Ingram, Richard T. *Ten Basic Responsibilities of Nonprofit Boards, Second Edition*. Washington, DC: BoardSource, 2009.
More than 150,000 board members have already discovered this #1 BoardSource bestseller. This revised edition explores the 10 core areas of board responsibility. Share with board members the basic responsibilities, including determining mission and purpose, ensuring effective planning, and participating in fundraising. You'll find that this is an ideal reference for drafting job descriptions, assessing board performance, and orienting board members on their responsibilities.

Mintz, Joshua and Jane Pierson. *Assessment of the Chief Executive: A Tool for Nonprofit Boards,* Revised. Washington, DC: BoardSource, 2005.
By failing to adequately evaluate the chief executive, many nonprofit boards miss an opportunity to express support for the executive and strengthen his or her performance. This resource provides a comprehensive tool boards can use in the evaluation process. After discussing the benefits of assessment, the user's guide suggests a process and provides a questionnaire that addresses every major area of responsibility. Also included is a self-evaluation form for the executive to complete and share with the board. This resource is also available in a quick and easy-to-use online version.

Moyers, Richard L. *The Nonprofit Chief Executive's Ten Basic Responsibilities.* Washington, DC: BoardSource, 2006.
As a companion to *Ten Basic Responsibilities of Nonprofit Boards,* this book was created to examine the chief executive's responsibilities — including supervising staff, overseeing operations, and supporting the board — through the same lens as those of the board. Different than a traditional management guide, this resource seeks to clarify the chief executive's role in the context of the necessary partnership with the board.

Ober|Kaler, attorneys at law. *The Nonprofit Legal Landscape.* Washington, DC: BoardSource, 2005.
Designed for executives and board members, *The Nonprofit Legal Landscape* explains the laws and legal concepts that affect nonprofit organizations. It serves as a handy reference tool for laws specific to tax exemption and for those regulating general business practices. When confronted with legal questions, nonprofit leaders can use this easy-to-read resource to rise rapidly to the next level of understanding.

Quatt, Charles W. and Brian Vogel. *Nonprofit Executive Compensation: Planning, Performance, and Pay, Second Edition.* Washington, DC: BoardSource, 2010.
Nonprofit chief executive compensation is coming under increasing scrutiny by the IRS, state regulators, the media, legislators, and potential funders. Does your board have a process that allows you to offer a salary that will attract and keep top talent without compromising your organization's mission or the public's expectations? This practical step-by-step guide and reference will help you establish an effective compensation structure. It will also help you maintain public trust by increasing the transparency and integrity of your compensation practices.

Tebbe, Don. *Chief Executive Transitions: How to Hire and Support a Nonprofit CEO.* Washington, DC: BoardSource, 2008.

When a nonprofit finds itself in need of a new chief executive, managing the transition effectively is crucial to the organization's future impact and continued success. Properly handled, the process can be an opportunity to enhance the organization and add to its effectiveness. This book will not only help boards navigate the hiring process but also oversee a successful leadership transition.

Trower, Cathy A. *Govern More, Manage Less: Harnessing the Power of Your Nonprofit Board, Second Edition.* Washington, DC: BoardSource, 2010.

Is your board managing instead of governing? Understanding this distinction will increase your board's ability to work effectively. Discover how your board can successfully work with staff, and how this dynamic changes as the size of your organization's staff changes. Also included are specific procedures to strengthen your board's capacity to govern.

Waechter, Susan A. *Driving Strategic Planning: A Nonprofit Executive's Guide, Second Edition.* Washington, DC: BoardSource, 2010.

This book will help you learn how to work with your staff and board to assess the readiness of your organization and prepare for strategic planning. Discover a variety of approaches for dealing with common issues and overcoming organizational resistance to beginning the process. Review the fundamental elements of the strategic planning process, from mission and vision to environmental scan and competitive analysis.

ABOUT THE AUTHORS

Sherill K. Williams has served as president and CEO of Prevent Blindness Ohio since 1986. Working in concert with a 35-member board of directors, her responsibilities are to coordinate a paid staff of 25, and 3,600 volunteers across Ohio, in implementing sight-saving programming by providing direct services to more than 800,000 Ohioans annually and educating millions of consumers about what they can do to protect and preserve their gift of sight. Prior to joining the staff of PBO, Sherry served as national director of youth volunteers for the March of Dimes Birth Defects Foundation from 1978–85, and as executive director of the Fairfield County, Conn., chapter of the March of Dimes in 1986.

Sherry is currently a trustee of GroundworkGroup, a member of the Ohio Association of Nonprofit Organization's Standards of Excellence Advisory Committee, and Ohio Women in Government. Additionally, she serves as an advisor for the Ann Ellis Fund of The Columbus Foundation and is a founding member of SOS (Save Our Sight) Coalition, Ohio Eye Care Coalition, and Ohio Aging Eye Public Private Partnership.

Sherry was inducted into the National Leadership Hall of Fame, Future Homemakers of America, and has received other honors and recognition, including the Outstanding Alumni Achievement Award from the Minnesota State Future Homemakers of America, Inc., Partner in Education Award from the New York City Board of Education, and National Distinguished Volunteer Service Award from the March of Dimes Birth Defects Foundation. She is a graduate of Leadership Columbus and served as a commissioner for the International Year of the Child Presidential National Commission in Washington, D.C.

Sherry holds a bachelor of arts degree in speech/communication from the University of Minnesota and a master's degree in public administration/health care administration from Pace University of New York.

Kathleen A. McGinnis has more than 25 years of experience directing all aspects of human resources, training, leadership, and organizational development in major retail and food service businesses. In her current consulting role, she focuses organizations toward achieving overall objectives by integrating human resources opportunities with strategic business plans. She partners with senior management to build cultures that enhance talent identification and development, retain quality employees at all levels, and incorporate people practices that directly contribute to overall profitability. Kathy's practice is focused on both for-profit and not-for-profit organizations.

Prior to embarking on a career in consulting, Kathy was executive vice president of human resources and training for Wendy's International Inc. She served as a member of the strategic planning council and participated in developing initiatives to re-energize the Wendy's brand and assimilate new business opportunities. Previously, Kathy also held vice president–level positions within the human resources and training areas with Gold Circle Stores, a former division of Federated Department Stores.

Kathy has significant experience in nonprofit board service, including serving as a founding board member and program chair for the R. David Thomas Foundation for Adoption, honorary board member and past chair of Prevent Blindness Ohio, board member and chair of the field relations committee for Prevent Blindness America, vice chair and human resources chair for Catholic Social Services, chair of the board for Friendship Village of Dublin, and member of the Advisory Board for WOSU. She is also an active volunteer for Life Care Alliance through the Meals on Wheels and Help at Home initiatives.

Kathy holds a bachelor of arts degree with a double major in English and psychology from Southern Illinois University. She was named hospitality motivator of the year, an industry award recognizing individuals who set new standards of excellence in the human resources field, in 1996 at the Elliot Conference. She has completed The President's Institute sponsored by The Academy for Leadership and Governance for Leaders of Nonprofit Boards in Central Ohio.